200+ Ideas
for Teaching Preschoolers

Published by New Hope
P. O. Box 12065
Birmingham, Alabama 35202-2065

© 1986 by New Hope
All rights reserved. Ninth printing 1998.
Printed in the United States of America.

ISBN: 0-936625-06-6
N868111•0802•3M12

Contents

Art — pages 5-18

Nighttime Pictures
Booklet of My Favorite Things
Self Art
Texture Boards
Sponge Shoe-Liner Prints
Seasonal Pictures
Frosty Painting
Pine Needle Painting
Prayer Reminders
Sparkle Designs
Object Printing
A Homemade Helping Tree
Trees
Paper-Plate Puppets
Foam Hamburger-Carton Puppets
Easel Paper Cut in Shapes
Squiggle Painting

Binoculars
Puff Painting
Surprise Play Dough
Yarn Sculpture
Sewing
Building a Church
Colored Sand
Ice Cube Painting
Aluminum Foil/Warmer Tray Pictures
Experimenting with Color
Egg-Shell Flowers
Rock Painting
Egg-Carton Caterpillars
Newspaper Art
Soap Crayons
Blob Painting
Simple Stained Glass

Stained-Glass Windows
Texture Center
Egg-Shell Collage
Napkin Holder
Napkin Rings
Christmas Tree Decoration
Christmas Finger Print Card
Personalized Christmas Tree Ornament
Shrink Art Christmas Ornament
Cornstarch Clay for Christmas Ornament
Leaf Prints
Finger-Paint/Tissue-Paper Pictures
Glue Paint
Cornstarch Paint
Flour Paste
Finger Paint

Homeliving — pages 19-26

Recipe Box Play
Pilgrim/Nurse's Hat
Playing Doctor and Nurse
Let's Go to Church
Bathtime
Sewing on Burlap
Compare Fresh Orange with Mandarin
Sorting, Matching, Folding
Missionary Paper Dolls

Meat-Tray Sewing Cards
Container for Candy, Cookies, or Plants
Dishes
Place Mats for Setting the Table
Sewing Cards
Easy-to-Dress Sunsuit for Doll
Fruit Salad
Skillet and Dustpan
Mailbox

Needlepoint
Multiuse Homeliving Toy
Shopping at the Grocery Store
Painted Cookies
Window Poster
Pouring and Measuring
Dress Closet

Nature — pages 27-36

Fun in the Wind
Fruits, Vegetables, and Their Seeds
Experiences with a Coconut
Observing Bean Seeds
Observing Gourds
Backpacking
Identify Smells
Easy Watering Cups
Bug Bottle
Find Out About Air
Whose House Is This?
Whose Home Is This?

Nature-in-a-Book
God Planned for Me Through Plants and Animals
Seed Book
Feeding Birds on a String
Matching Game: Seeds
A Bottle's Eye View
Worms Are Useful
Artificial Snow
Ocean in a Bottle
Animal Tracks
Discovering a Rainbow

A Trip to the Farm
Nature Album
Tasting Pineapple
Identify Sounds
Nature Walk
Sunny/Rainy Reversible Pictures
Sounds
Animal Homes Sorting Game
Object Match
Colored Bubbles
A Nature Frieze
Showing Slides

Puzzles — pages 37-41

Tube and Spool Puzzle
Key Match
Feel and Match
Paper-Plate Puzzles
Cookie-Sheet Puzzle
Objects Puzzle

Puzzle in a File Folder
Flower Puzzles
Make a Picture
Puzzle Book
Choose and Guess
Match the Pictures

What Goes Together?
Concentration/Two-of-a-Kind
Smile or Frown Decision Game
Pairs of Things

Music

pages 42-48

Teaching Songs Through Pictures
Song: "Thank You, Jesus, for Our Food"
Song: "This Is the Way"
Making a Drum
Rhythms
Paper-Plate Shakers

Making Rhythm Sticks
Two Sounds See-Through Shaker Shakers
Creative Streamers
Downbeat
Turtle Walk
Ham-Can Banjo

Movement Patterns
Who's Got the Chicken?
Who's Got the Egg?
Feel the Beat
Dial a Song
Driving Along the Highway
Action Songs Using Familiar Tunes

Games

pages 49-56

It's Me
The Color Game
Hot or Cold Climates
Name the Animal
Mystery Sock Box
Tube Pumping
Who Will Ride the Train?
Choosing a Song or Prayer Request
Spin the Can
Tell a Story

Ways Missionaries Travel
Riddle Game
Fishing
Box-Ball-Action
Hello!
Pretend and Stretch
Egg Carton-Numeral Recognition
Concentration
Hiding Snowballs
Relaxing

Music Mirroring
The Color of My Clothes
Kick the Jug
Look at Me
Adam and Eve (Finger Play)
Relaxation
Picture-Cube Toss
Guess the Instrument
Wiggle Game
Colors

Recipes

pages 57-62

Chinese Ting-a-Lings
Doughnuts
Biscuit Pizza
Gingerbread People
Brazilian Baked Bananas
Animal-Cracker Sandwiches
Making Pudding
Creamy Candy

Peanut Butter
Easy Candy
Peanut Butter Balls
No-Bake Peanut Butter Cookies
Cup-Cake Cones
Banana Smoothie
Bananas and Granola
Applesauce

Homemade Snowcone
Easy Chocolate Ice Cream
No-Bake Oatmeal Cookies
Orange Juice Drink
Hot Chocolate Mix Gift Jars
Kenyan Corn Cakes
Graham-Cracker Balls

Enrichment Ideas

pages 63-72

Book for Infants and Creepers
Fishing
Changeable Mobile
Wooden Tugboat, Cabin Cruiser, and Van
City Scene
Fence
Writing a Story
Design Board
Quiet Book
Changeable Book for Younger Preschoolers
Plastic Book for Younger Preschoolers

Photograph-Album Book for Young Ones
Helpers-at-Church Book
Push and Crawl Toy
Jeans Chair
Beginning Sounds
Match Shape Silhouettes
Homemade Bubbles
Racquet and Ball
Peekaboo Board
Mobile for Creepers and Toddlers
Easel
How to Laminate Inexpensively

Handy Picture File
Workbench Substitute
The Street Where I Go to Church
Listening Glasses
Doll Cradle
Matching Block Patterns
Toe Toucher
Treasure Box
Storage Boxes
Let's Go Camping

200+ Ideas
for Teaching
Preschoolers

Art

"Let me do it myself."

Nighttime Pictures

Materials: sponges cut into star and moon shapes; clothespins; black or dark blue construction paper; white and yellow tempera paint; disposable pie pans

An adult should cut sponges into star and moon shapes. Preschooler will stamp designs, as for object printing, using white or yellow paint. This process may be repeated until child completes the nighttime picture.

—Submitted by Sharon B. Garnett
Chesapeake, Virginia

Booklet of *My Favorite Things*

Materials: pictures of toys, foods, clothes, pets, houses, cars, flowers, and people; white typing paper (8½-by-11 inches); stapler with staples; yarn or brads; bright-colored construction paper; and a hole punch

Suggest that preschoolers find pictures of their favorite things. Lead them to paste the pictures on white typing paper, one picture on each page. Staple pages together to make a booklet. (Holes may be punched and booklet put together with yarn or brads.) Use two sheets of construction paper for a cover for the booklet. A teacher prints *My Favorite Things* on the front cover.

—Submitted by Christine McCauley
Tallahassee, Florida

Self Art

Materials: wall mirror and water-based felt-tip markers

Lead the child to stand in front of a wall or freestanding mirror. Provide several colors of markers. Include a color the child is wearing. Guide the child to choose a color and mark on the mirror. The child may try to outline himself as he discovers his image or he may enjoy creating his own designs. This should be the child's choice.

—Submitted by Peggy Ward
Vicksburg, Mississippi

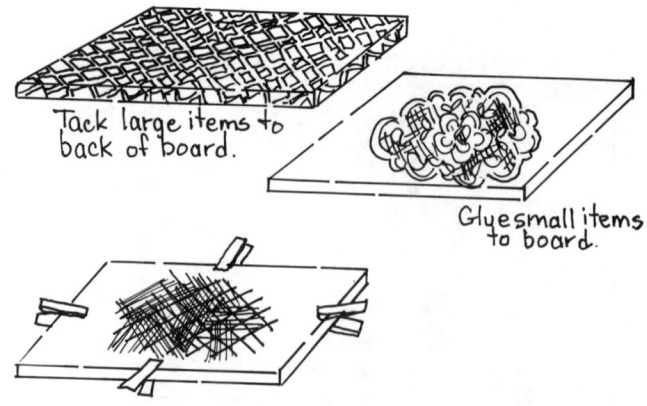

Texture Boards

Materials: several pieces of 12-by-15-inch lightweight wood or heavy cardboard; different textures of fabric (net, corduroy); plastic doilies; textured bathtub designs; mesh produce bag; textured wallpaper designs; newsprint; spring-type clothespins; and large crayons

Glue or tack the items to the boards in advance. Remove the paper covering from the crayons so the side of the crayon may be used. Instruct the child to place the newsprint over the cardboard that has the textured items on it. Hold the paper in place with clothespins. Let the child rub the crayon over the paper and watch the design come through the newsprint.

—Submitted by Mary Johnson
Lousiville, Kentucky

Sponge Shoe-Liner Prints

Materials: one package flat sponge shoe liners cut into shapes (flowers, heart, butterfly)

An adult should cut shapes out of the shoe liners. Glue each shape to a wooden block or spool. Preschooler will stamp designs as for object printing. The holes in the sponge liner give an interesting design.

—Submitted by Carolyn Hatcher
Dunwoody, Georgia

Seasonal Pictures

Materials: cotton, construction paper, twigs, white tempera paint, cotton swabs, and disposable pie pans

Winter

Talk to the preschoolers about winter, snow, bare trees, etc. Give each preschooler a piece of dark blue construction paper, cotton, cotton swabs, glue, and twigs from outdoors. Lead the preschoolers to glue cotton to construction paper to look like snow, glue twigs on paper to represent trees, dip cotton swab in white tempera paint and dab on paper to represent snow falling.

Autumn

Provide red, orange, yellow, green, and brown tempera paint. Suggest that autumn pictures be made with the cotton swabs.

—Submitted by Sharon B. Garnett
Chesapeake, Virginia
and
B. Kittrell
Mobile, Alabama

Frosty Painting

Materials: 12-by-18-inch paper; crayons; very thick consistency of white tempera mixed with liquid detergent; brushes; and comb or notched cardboard

Color the entire surface of the paper using the sides of the crayons and pressing down heavily. Paint over the entire surface with a thick tempera mixture. Allow the paint to dry. Pull a comb or notched piece of cardboard over the painting. The colors are revealed, making a variegated pattern.

—Submitted by Nina Joseph
Mobile, Alabama

Pine Needle Painting

Materials: several small pine limbs with green needles, liquid tempera paint, two disposable pie pans, and large newsprint

Mix a different color of paint in each of the pie pans. Encourage the preschoolers to dip the pine needles in the paint and brush back and forth, just like a paintbrush. What fun!

—Submitted by Maxine Sparks
Charlotte, North Carolina

Prayer Reminders

Materials: four-by-six-inch index cards; felt-tip markers or crayons; and the name of a missionary

Make a one-week calendar for each child. Print the name of a missionary on each child's calendar. Lead the child to decorate his calendar, leaving the days blank. Tell the child to take the calendar home as a prayer reminder. Each day he prays for the missionary, he may color that square or use a sticker to place on that day.

—Submitted by Barbara Parker
Pineville, North Carolina

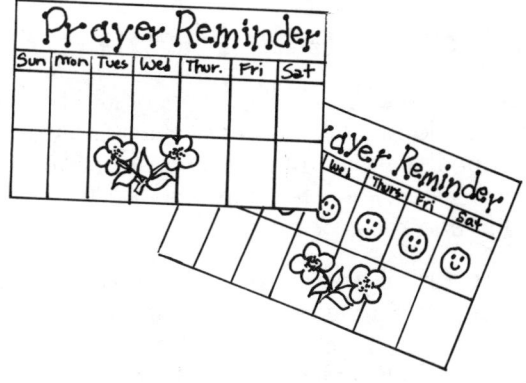

Sparkle Designs

Materials: flour, salt, water, heavy plastic-coated paper plates, three plastic containers, three colors of dry tempera, and three spoons

Mix equal parts of flour, salt, and water. If necessary, add more water to make a thin consistency. Divide mixture into three separate containers. Add a different color of dry tempera to each mixture. Drop a spoonful of each mixture onto a plate. Lead the child to tilt the paper plate from side to side to allow the colors to run together to make a beautiful design. Allow the painting to dry. Salt makes the design glisten.

—Submitted by Susan Maund
Ozark, Alabama

Object Printing

Materials: newsprint or manila paper; a collection of small household objects, such as empty spools, plastic forks, cardboard tubes, corks, small blocks, hair rollers, corrugated paper, pencil erasers, sponge pieces, plastic kitchen scrubber, small glass, etc.; felt pieces; tempera paint; and several small disposable pie pans

Make two or three simple stamp pads for printing by cutting felt or a sponge to fit into the bottom of each pie pan. Prepare a thick mixture of two or three colors of tempera paint. Pour just enough of a color into a pie pan to soak into the felt or sponge.

Give each preschooler a sheet of paper. Lead each one to choose an object to press on a stamp pad, then on his paper. Allow him to experiment and create his own designs by trying different objects and different colors.

—Submitted by Mrs. R. L. Blaine
Bowling Green, Kentucky

A Homemade Helping Tree

Materials: tree branch; flower pot or tall can; spray paint or florist's foil; plaster of Paris; individually-wrapped candy; ribbon, construction-paper circles with Bible thoughts and stickers; paper chain; and rocks or sand

Select a small tree branch. Place it in a can or flower pot. Fill the can or pot with rocks or sand to hold the branch upright. Pour a mixture of plaster of Paris over the top of the rocks to seal.

Trees

Materials: paper cups, craft sticks, wood shavings, seeds, glue, and construction paper

Cut each paper cup in half vertically. Give each child one half of a paper cup and a piece of paper. Lead the child to glue the cup to the lower center of the paper (flat-side-down). Guide the preschooler to arrange craft sticks in the cup to represent tree limbs. Glue the sticks to the paper, then lead him to arrange wood shavings and seeds around the top of the sticks.

Talk about how trees help people. They are used for shade, food, climbing, homes for birds and other animals, firewood, etc.

—Submitted by Pamela Hiles
Fort Worth, Texas

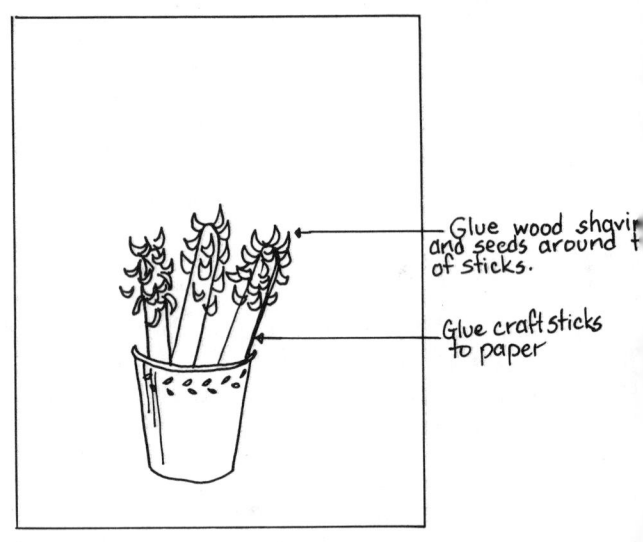

Spray the branch and can with paint, or cover the pot with florist's foil.

Lead some preschoolers to make tree decorations from construction-paper circles by pasting on Bible thoughts and pictures. Lead some preschoolers to make paper chains by using strips of paper on which Bible thoughts have been printed.

Fasten the decorations to the tree with ribbon. Individually-wrapped candies may be added, if

Paper-Plate Puppets

Materials: paper plates; construction-paper scraps; white paste; craft sticks; crayons or felt-tip markers; yarn; and glue

Lead the child to draw a face on the plate using crayons or felt-tip markers. Child may prefer to make the face by gluing on construction-paper pieces. Attach a craft stick to the bottom of the plate to use as a handle.

Plate puppets can be used in dramatic play. The child may hold the plate in front of his face to repeat a Bible verse, sing a song, answer a question, or pretend to be a missionary or Bible character.

—Submitted by Millie Mullock
Columbia, South Carolina

Foam Hamburger-Carton Puppets

Materials: one Styrofoam hamburger carton for each puppet; crayons or permanent felt-tip markers; glue; yarn; and scissors

Lead preschooler to draw a face on the top of the carton. Explain that the opening of the carton is the mouth. Lead the child to draw the mouth above and below the opening. Cut hair from yarn. Glue hair to the carton.

Lead the preschooler to use the puppet to recall a story, respond to a question, or engage in a conversation.

—Submitted by Nell Branum
Mount Olive, Alabama

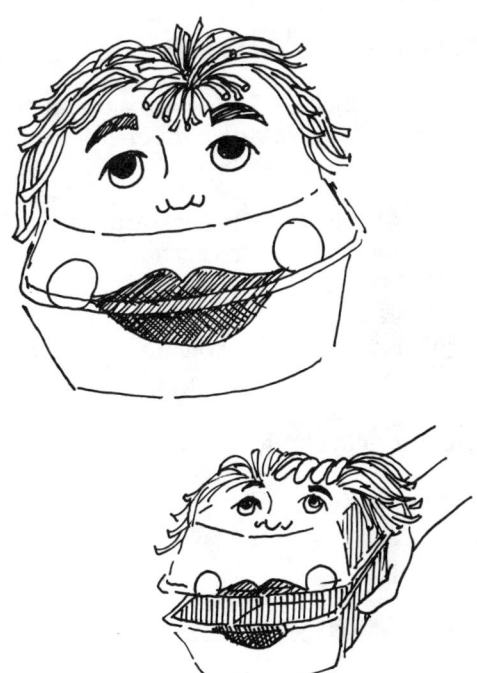

appropriate. Take the branch to a nursing home or hospital for people to enjoy.

—Submitted by Marlene Parker
Bixby, Oklahoma

Easel Paper Cut in Shapes

Materials: easel-size newsprint; scissors; tempera paints; paintbrushes; and painting smocks

Cut a hole in a sheet of easel paper (any size or shape, any place on the paper). Attach the paper to an easel. Observe how the child uses the hole in the paper. Some preschoolers will incorporate the hole into a design or picture. Others will ignore the hole.
Note: Easel paper may be cut also in the shape of a butterfly, a church, a house, etc.

—Submitted by Myra Adams
Hurst, Texas

Puff Painting

Materials: shaving cream; smocks, vinyl cloth or waterproof tabletop; large meat trays or cafeteria trays; and damp paper towels

Cover a child's clothes with a smock. Lead the child to sit or stand at a table. Place a meat tray or cafeteria tray on the table in front of the child. Put a puff of shaving cream on the tray. Instruct the child to use fingers, fists, and wrists to move the puff of shaving cream around to make different shapes. Fingers may be used to make lines and squiggles in the puff.

Use paper towels to clean hands and table for next child.

—Submitted by Kaye Riggs
Houston, Texas

Squiggle Painting

Materials: 14-inch pieces of yarn, construction paper, and three colors of tempera paint in three containers

Ask the child to fold the construction paper in half, creasing it on the fold. Then open it out flat. Lead him to dip a piece of yarn into a container of paint. He then places the yarn on one side of the construction paper, allowing an end to extend out at the bottom. Have him refold the paper. As he holds down the paper with one hand, he pulls the yarn from the bottom, squiggling it as he pulls.

He opens the paper to see the design. He may repeat the process with another color of paint.

—Submitted by Jeanne Lou Pile
Knoxville, Tennessee

Binoculars

Materials: toilet-tissue rolls; masking tape, yarn; and crayons, felt-tip markers, or tempera paint with brushes

Lead the preschooler to tape two tissue rolls close together at each end, leaving approximately one-half inch between rolls. Punch a hole in each side of one end to thread the yarn through for a neck strap. Knot the yarn inside the rolls. Lead the child to decorate the binoculars with crayons, felt-tip markers, or tempera paint. (If tempera paint is used, when completed, spray with hair spray to prevent paint from rubbing off.)

Talk about all the things God made that they can see through the binoculars. You may go for a nature walk to make discoveries.

—Submitted by Myra Adams
Hurst, Texas

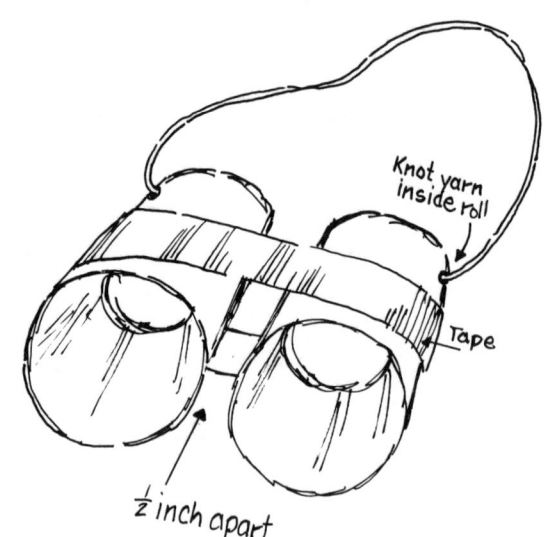

Surprise Play Dough

Materials: one cup flour, one cup water, one-half cup salt, one tablespoon oil, two teaspoons cream of tartar, and food coloring

Mix together all ingredients, except food coloring. Cook, stirring constantly, until the mixture pulls away from the side of the pan. Pour the mixture onto waxed paper and knead. Mold the white dough into six round, medium-sized balls. Use a finger to make a deep hole in each ball. Put a drop or two of food coloring into each hole. A different color may be used in each ball. Gently cover the hole without squeezing the ball.

Give each ball of play dough to a child. As the child squeezes the ball and works the dough with his hands, the color appears. Preschoolers enjoy watching the play dough change color.

Note: Play dough may be made in advance and kept in an airtight container.

—Submitted by Selma Johnson
Shreveport, Louisiana

Yarn Sculpture

Materials: different colors of yarn, small bowl, liquid starch, and waxed paper

Dip various lengths of yarn into a bowl of liquid starch. Let the yarn drip a few seconds. Lead the child to arrange the yarn in a pattern on a piece of waxed paper. Other pieces of yarn may be added in the same manner, crossing over and around the first piece. When the yarn is dry, the child will peel it from the waxed paper to discover a yarn sculpture.

—Submitted by Hilda Dalzell
Lexington, Kentucky

Sewing

Materials: 12-inch squares of burlap; 18-inch lengths of different colored yarn; and large, plastic tapestry needles

Machine stitch the edges of the burlap using a zigzag stitch. Tape or glue one end of each strand of yarn. Give each preschooler one square of burlap and a needle threaded with yarn. Guide the child to stitch a design. The taped end of the yarn will keep yarn from pulling through the burlap. When the child finishes with one color of yarn, allow him to choose another color. The teacher will need to thread needles and tie knots.

—Submitted by Martha Harless
Enid, Oklahoma

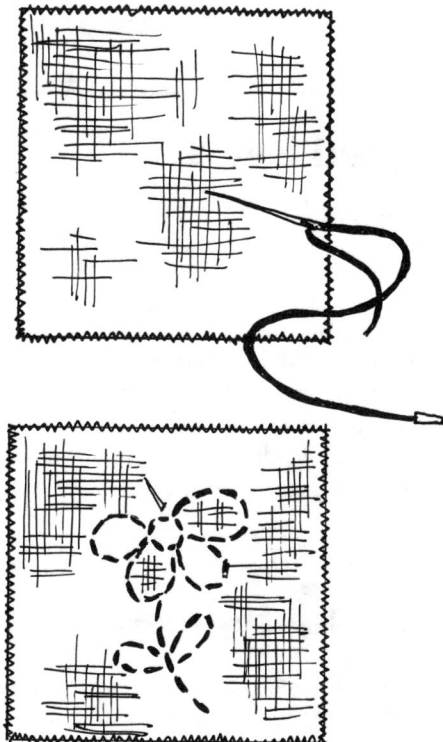

Building a Church

Materials: colored construction paper cut in five-eighths-by-three-inch rectangles and five-eighths-by-five-inch rectangles; glue or paste; large sheets of manila paper or light-colored construction paper; and crayons or felt-tip markers

Place colored construction-paper strips in a container, such as a box lid. Guide the preschooler to use the strips to build a church by gluing strips on a large sheet of construction paper. He may make doors and windows with crayons or felt-tip markers.

—Submitted by Mrs. Fred Halbrooks
Louisville, Kentucky

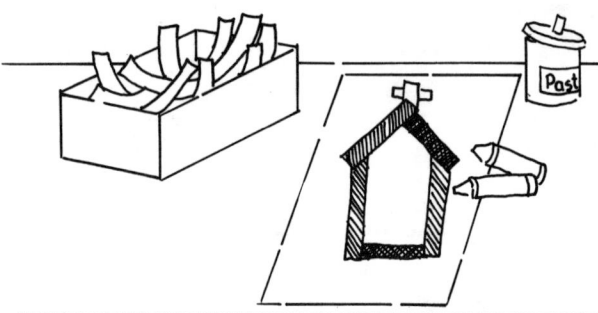

Colored Sand

Materials: dry fine-grain sand, shaker bottle, dry tempera paint, construction paper, glue, glue brush, and newspaper

Mix one or two teaspoons of dry tempera with the sand in a shaker bottle. Guide the preschooler to draw a picture with glue and a brush. Lead him to shake the colored sand over his paper. Allow the glue to dry. Then guide the preschooler to shake the excess sand onto the newspaper.

—Submitted by Carolyn Hatcher
Dunwoody, Georgia

Ice Cube Painting

Materials: smocks, manila paper, ice cubes, newspaper, and dry tempera paint in salt shakers

Cover the table with newspaper. Put a smock on each child. Lead the preschooler to sprinkle dry tempera from the shaker onto the manila paper, then use the ice cube to spread the paint. Lead the child to repeat this action using as many colors as he desires for as long as he likes.

—Submitted by Steve Peek
Knoxville, Tennessee

Aluminum Foil/Warmer Tray Pictures

Materials: warmer tray; aluminum foil; crayons with paper removed; and cooking mitt

Turn the warmer tray to low heat. Cut about a 9-by-12-inch piece of foil and place it on the tray. Lead the child to use the mitt to hold the tray with one hand. Guide him to use the other hand to draw a picture on the foil, moving the crayons slowly so that the tip will melt as it moves to produce a beautiful color. It's fun to experiment.
  Note: Tray will not be hot enough to burn a child, but it will get very warm. Be sure to use the cooking mitt. Provide close supervision.

—Submitted by Carolyn Hatcher
Dunwoody, Georgia

Experimenting with Color

Materials: cotton swabs, three or four small plastic containers, three colors of dry tempera paint, water, and newsprint

Place about two tablespoons of a different color of dry tempera in each of three small plastic containers. Fill a container about one-fourth full of water. Lead the preschooler to dip a cotton swab into the water, then into a color of dry tempera, then spread it over the newsprint. Repeat this action using all of the colors and mixing colors on the newsprint. Preschoolers will enjoy the effects of all the different colors they can make.

—Submitted by Linda Wayne
Ozark, Alabama

Egg-Shell Flowers

Materials: crushed egg shells, colored pink, yellow, blue, violet, and green; manila paper; glue; cotton swabs; jar lids; small disposable pie pans; and a large, flat pan with sides

Draw flowers. Dip a cotton swab in glue in a jar lid, and paint glue on the leaves. Sprinkle green egg shells on, then shake excess into pan. Paint petals of the flowers with glue and sprinkle with the pastel-colored egg shells. Then shake off the excess into the pan.

—Submitted by Wilma Davis
Marshall, Texas

Rock Painting

Materials: assorted collections of rocks; felt-tip markers or tempera paint and brushes; aerosol hair spray; newspaper; and smocks

Cover the table with newspaper. Place rocks on the table. Put a smock on each child. Guide each child to select a rock. Lead the child to use felt-tip markers or paint to draw designs on the rocks.

Allow the rocks to dry. Spray the rocks with hair spray so paint will not rub off.

Rocks may be used as paperweights, given as gifts, or saved as collectibles.

—Submitted by Cris Williamson
Macon, Georgia

Egg-Carton Caterpillars

Materials: picture of caterpillar; one egg carton for two preschoolers; one chenille stem per child; scissors; crayons or permanent felt-tip markers; and stick-on colored dots or construction-paper scraps and glue

Display a picture of a caterpillar. Cut each egg carton in half lengthwise. Give each child a half of an egg carton. Lead him to turn the carton upside down. Show him the humps of the caterpillar. Lead the child to make the antennae by inserting the chenille stem into the egg carton at one end. Suggest that the child use crayons or permanent felt-tip markers to draw a face under the antennae. Lead the child to decorate the body of the caterpillar by gluing on small pieces of construction paper or using crayons or stick-on colored dots. Note: Some crayons will not mark well on plastic foam egg cartons.

—Submitted by Nell Branum
Mount Olive, Alabama

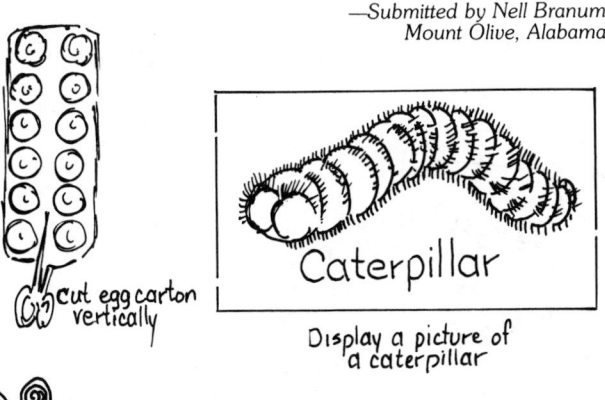

Newspaper Art

Materials: classified section of the newspaper, construction paper, and paste

Cut geometric shapes or shapes of objects from newspaper. Lead the boys and girls to create their newspaper art by pasting the shapes on the construction paper in whatever designs they choose.

—Submitted by Christine McCauley
Tallahassee, Florida

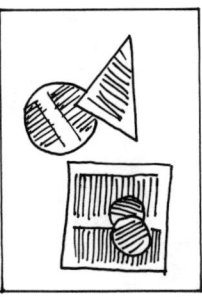

Soap Crayons

Materials: red, blue, and yellow food coloring; one-fourth cup water; one and three-fourths cups soap powder; a measuring cup; muffin tins; vegetable oil; spoon; sponges; and paper towels

Put soap powder and water in a pan. Mix together until lumps are gone. Divide the mixture into three equal parts. Add food coloring to each part (three colors). Press mixture into oiled muffin tins. Allow to dry and harden several days.

Lead the preschooler to draw pictures and designs on windows in the room. When finished, provide sponges and paper towels to clean the windows. (Soap crayons can also be used to paint child's face as a clown.)

Blob Painting

Materials: yellow and purple tempera paint (mix to thick consistency); white or pastel construction paper; and spoon or tongue depressor

Lead the child to fold paper in half and crease it. Then open it again. Drop a small amount of each color paint from a spoon or tongue depressor onto the paper. Then refold the paper. Press it together, then open it. See the beautiful shapes that are formed.

—Submitted by Oleta P. Meares
Lumberton, North Carolina

Simple Stained Glass

Materials: white typing paper; cooking or mineral oil; cotton swabs; wax crayons; yarn; and black tempera paint

Lead the child to paint a picture or design on the paper using black tempera paint. With a cotton swab or fingers, let him spread cooking oil over all the paper until covered. Allow the oil to soak in, then wipe off excess oil until the paper is translucent, and dry. The preschooler then colors both sides of the paper with the crayons.

This makes a beautiful hanging for a window, or it may be shared with someone who is sick or someone in a nursing home.

—Submitted by Lou Crussel
Coweta, Oklahoma

Stained-Glass Windows

Materials: crayon shavings, waxed paper, iron, cardboard frames cut in window shapes, newspaper, scissors, newsprint, and glue

Cut waxed paper into six-inch squares. Place one square on a thick layer of newspaper. Lead the preschooler to spread two pinches of crayon shavings over the waxed paper square. Place another waxed paper square over the crayons. Place newsprint on top and press with a fairly hot iron, working from the center out to seal the edges. Tape each design to a cardboard frame.

—Submitted by Jan Morris
Tulsa, Oklahoma

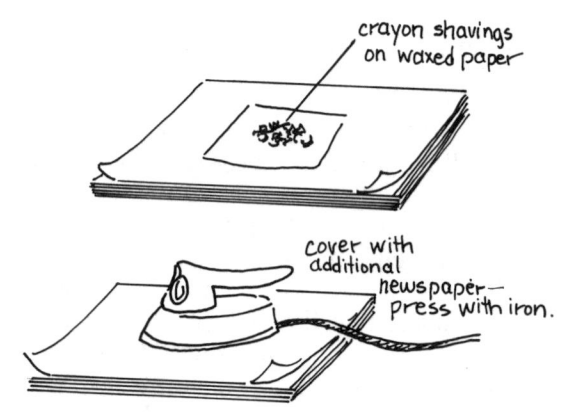

Texture Center

Materials: ten squares of four-by-four-inch poster board; assorted textured items, such as sandpaper, buttons, paper clips, corduroy, yarn, cotton, screws, foil, and rope; scissors; glue; box; and blindfold

Give each child two squares of poster board. Ask each child to select an item from the assortment of articles. Lead each child to glue the item to a square of poster board. Then lead him to make another identical square.

Put all of the squares into a box. Shake the box to mix the squares.

Blindfold one child at a time. Chose a square from the box and put it in the blindfolded child's hand so that he can feel the texture. The child will use the other hand to search in the box for the identical square to match the one in his hand.

The preschoolers will take turns being blindfolded.

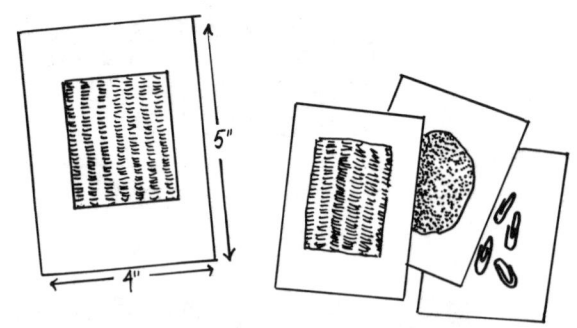

Egg-Shell Collage

Materials: clean, dry egg shells; water; jars; liquid measuring cup; food coloring; white glue; paper towels; manila paper or colored construction paper; and large box

Place egg shells in a large box on the floor or table. Guide preschoolers to take turns crushing them into tiny pieces (not powder). Put one cup of water in each jar. Add food coloring to the water, a different color to each jar. Put crushed egg shells into each jar and allow the shells to remain until the desired shade results. Drain off the water. Spread the tinted shells on paper towels to dry completely.

Give each preschooler a piece of paper. Guide each one to spread glue in patterns or outlines on the paper. Help them to drop colored shells on the glue, then gently shake off excess shells into a box.

Egg-Shell Vase

Cut the top off a detergent bottle. Cover the bottle with glue. Sprinkle egg shells onto the glue until bottle is completely covered. Allow vase to dry completely.

—Submitted by Nina Joseph
Mobile, Alabama

Napkin Rings

Materials: tissue or paper-towel tubes cut in one and-a-half-inch rings; glue; gift-wrapping paper; and scissors

Cut a piece of colorful gift-wrapping paper in four-by-six-inch pieces. Lead the preschooler to spread glue sparingly over the entire back of the paper. Place the cardboard ring on one edge of the paper and roll the paper around it. Push the extra paper inside the ring and smooth to seal.

These napkin rings may be given to elderly friends in nursing homes or used as tray favors in hospitals.

—Submitted by Jan Morris
Tulsa, Oklahoma

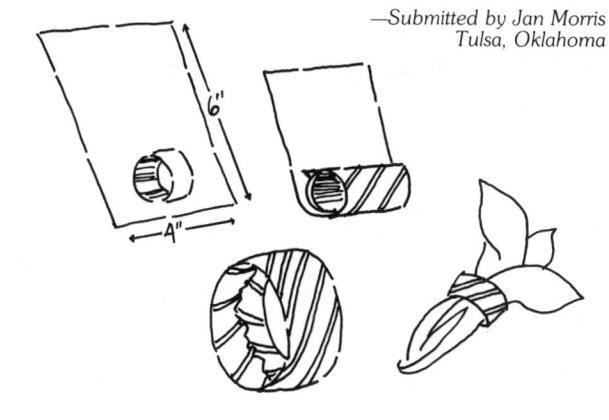

Napkin Holder

Materials: precut poster-board shapes, approximately four inches in size (hearts, Christmas trees, flowers, leaves, snowmen, etc.); appropriate items for decorations (confetti made with a hole punch, ribbon, crayons, wallpaper scraps, felt-tip markers, etc.); wooden spring-type clothespins; colorful napkins; and strong glue

Lead the preschoolers to decorate the poster-board shapes. Guide them to glue a clothespin to the back of the shape with the clip end down. Allow the glue to dry thoroughly. Help the preschoolers to fold the napkins and clip them into the holder. These make attractive and inexpensive gifts that preschoolers enjoy sharing with others.

—Submitted by Sue M. Perry
Gulfport, Mississippi

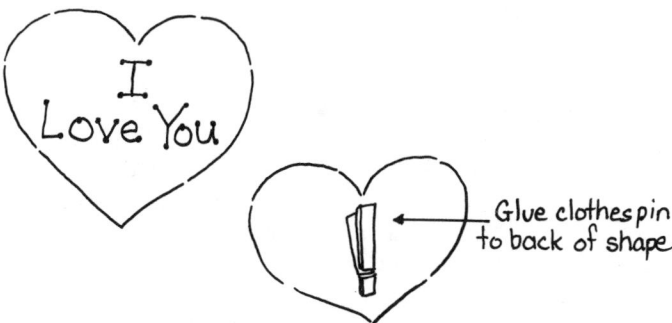

Christmas Tree Decoration

Materials: Styrofoam meat trays, decorative ribbon, scissors, and permanent felt-tip markers

A teacher should cut out bell and Christmas tree shapes from Styrofoam. Make a hole in the top of each one. Lead the child to use felt-tip markers to decorate each one. Place ornaments on a cookie sheet. Heat in a 200°F oven for one minute to shrink to miniature size. Put ribbon through hole and tie.

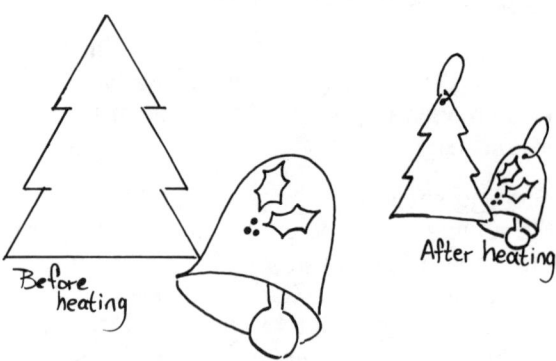

—Submitted by Del Lamb
Columbia, South Carolina

Christmas Finger Print Card

Materials: red and/or green ink pads and paper

Lead the child to press his fingers on the ink pad (made from green or red tempera paint poured over a sponge) and then to press them firmly on the paper. Fingers may be gently rolled back and forth to make a design. The child may make a star, a Christmas tree, or just make a design. Allow the child to be creative.

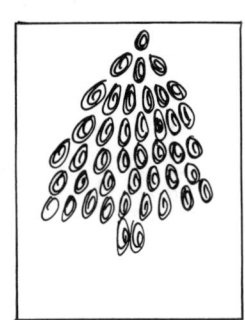

—Submitted by Brenda Dedmon
Snellville, Georgia

Personalized Christmas Tree Ornaments

Materials: construction paper; glitter or glitter glue; yarn; pencil; hole punch; and scissors

Print the child's first name in fairly-large letters on construction paper. Cut the name out and let the child trace the name with glue. Suggest that the child sprinkle the glitter over the outline and then shake off the excess. Put a hole in the construction paper where the child may thread the yarn through. Tie for hanging on the tree. This gives the tree a personal touch. Other shapes and symbols may also be used.

—Submitted by Betty West
Vinton, Virginia

Shrink Art Christmas Ornament

Materials: clear plastic delicatessen lids (from grocery store meat counters or delicatessen counters); hole punch; permanent felt-tip markers; red or green yarn; Christmas stencils; cookie sheet; and oven

Place stencil inside the rim of the plastic lid. Lead the child to color the shape with a felt-tip marker. Punch a hole near the top of the lid. Use a permanent felt-tip marker to print the child's name and the year at the bottom of the rim. Place the plastic lid on the cookie sheet. Put the cookie sheet in the oven. Bake at 300°F until the lid has totally flattened on the pan. The lid may curl up and stick together while shrinking. Separate it with a knife while it is still hot so it will flatten. Remove from the oven and cool. Remove ornament from the pan. Put a piece of yarn through the hole and tie. This will be a decoration the family will treasure.

Note: Plastic lids are different. Experiment with different kinds to determine which is best.

—Submitted by Steve Peek
Knoxville, Tennessee

Cornstarch Clay for Christmas Ornaments

Materials: one cup cornstarch; two cups baking soda; one and one-fourth cups water; pot and hot plate or electric skillet; spoon; measuring cups; plastic bag; rolling pin; and cookie cutters

Mix cornstarch, soda, and water in a pot or skillet. Cook and stir constantly until of mashed potato consistency. Knead. Store in a plastic bag until ready to use.

Lead the child to use a rolling pin to roll out the dough. The child will use cookie cutters to cut shapes. Punch a hole in the top of each shape. Put the child's initials on the back of each ornament. Allow ornament to dry (at least 24 hours), then turn it over and allow to completely dry. Preschoolers will use tempera paint to paint ornaments. When paint dries, spray each ornament with hair spray to prevent paint from rubbing off. Attach a string through the hole in the top by which to hang the ornament on the Christmas tree.

—Submitted by Carolyn Hatcher
Dunwoody, Georgia

Leaf Prints

Materials: fresh leaves (not dry, brittle ones); shoe polish or liquid tempera; manila paper; and cotton swabs or paintbrushes

Coat the vein side of a leaf with shoe polish or liquid tempera. Put the painted side of the leaf down on manila paper. Put another piece of paper on top of the leaf. Gently rub over the paper. Lift the top paper and the leaf to find a print. This process may be repeated for a child to have several different leaf prints on one sheet of paper.

—Submitted by Lou Crussel
Coweta, Oklahoma

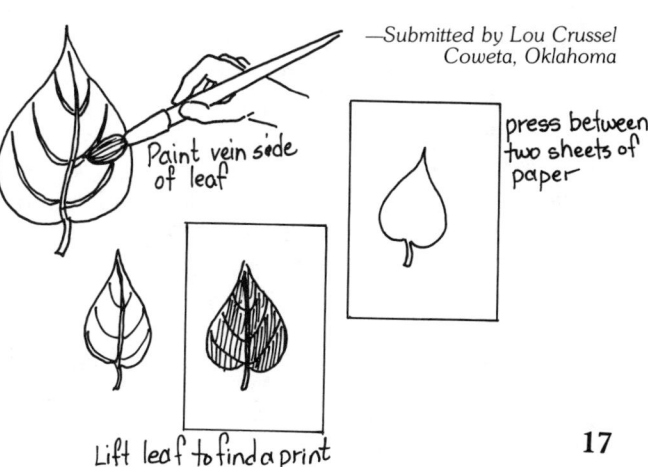

Finger-Paint/Tissue-Paper Pictures

Materials: finger-paint paper, finger paint, tissue paper, and scissors

The adult will cut shapes from tissue paper (hearts, flowers, bells, triangles, etc.). Sprinkle the finger-paint paper with a little water. Lead the child to spread the water to cover the entire sheet. Add a teaspoon of finger paint. Allow the child to finger paint until the entire sheet is covered. Give the child shapes cut from tissue paper. Lead the child to place the shapes on the paint while it is still wet. Allow pictures to dry.

—*Submitted by Carolyn Hatcher*
Dunwoody, Georgia

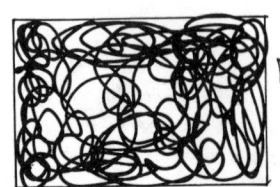

Finger paint until page is covered

Add tissue paper shapes

Glue Paint

Materials: white glue, dry tempera, and glitter

Add dry tempera to a small squeeze bottle of white glue. Shake or stir well to mix. Lead the child to draw a picture or design, then outline his drawing with tinted glue. Allow drawing to dry completely.

Preschoolers will enjoy the effect of the raised outlines as they run their fingers over them. Glitter may be added to the glue and applied in the same manner.

—*Submitted by Helen Posey*
Vicksburg, Mississippi

Flour Paste

Materials: one and one-half cups boiling water, one and one-half tablespoons powdered alum, three cups flour, three cups cold water, and one and one-half teaspoons oil of cloves

Add alum to the boiling water. Mix flour and cold water until smooth. Pour slowly into the boiling water. Cook until mixture turns bluish in color, stirring constantly. Remove from heat and add oil of cloves. Stir well. If too thick, add a little water. Put in airtight containers. This keeps well.

—*Submitted by Lou Crussel*
Coweta, Oklahoma

Cornstarch Paint

Materials: eight cups water, one cup cornstarch, and food coloring

Bring seven cups of water to a boil. Mix well, until smooth, one cup cold water and one cup cornstarch. Add to the boiling water, stirring constantly. Bring to a boil and remove from heat. Add food coloring for the desired color. Cool before using. If paint is too thick, add liquid starch. When not in use, store in a cool place or in the refrigerator. This makes good paint for preschoolers when tempera paint is not available.

—*Submitted by Lou Crussel*
Coweta, Oklahoma

Finger Paint

Materials: five cups hot water, two cups flour, one-half cup soap powder, one-half cup salt, saucepan, stove or hot plate, bowls or jars, several colors of dry tempera paint, and spoon

Cook the water and flour 15 minutes, stirring constantly. Remove from heat, add soap powder and salt. Divide into four pints. Add four tablespoons of tempera paint to each pint while hot (a different color to each pint). Add liquid starch if too stiff.

—*Submitted by Millie G. Mullock*
Columbia, South Carolina

Homeliving

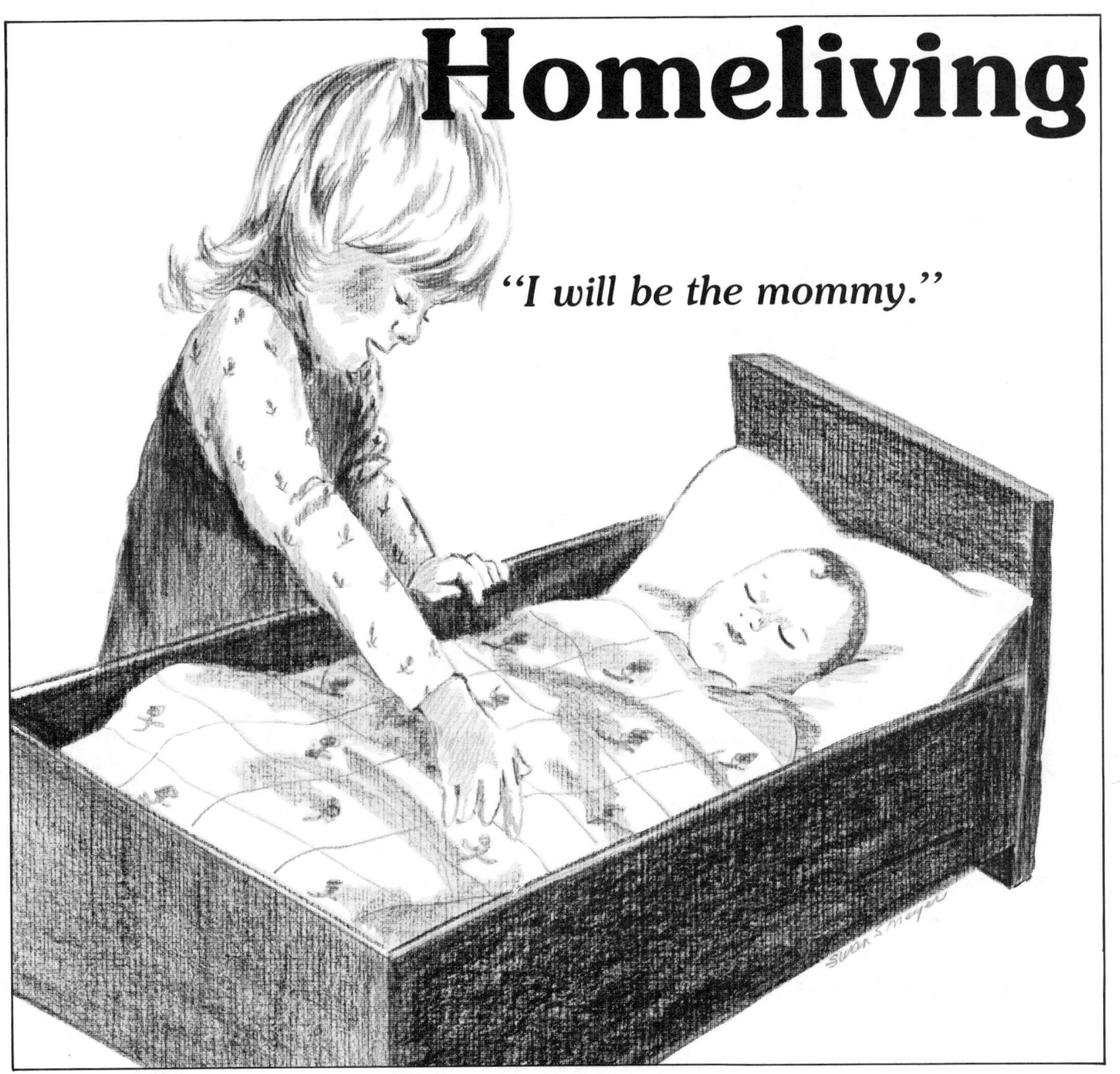

"I will be the mommy."

Recipe Box Play

Materials: recipe file box; pictures of vegetables, meats, and fruits (two each); glue; and blank recipe cards or index cards

Glue the pictures of foods on the recipe cards. Place the cards in the recipe box. Encourage the preschoolers to arrange the table with a tablecloth, placemats, dishes, and recipe cards. Use the recipe cards for pretend food on the plates or in other ways.

—Submitted by Lillian Hill
Waco, Texas

Pilgrim/Nurse's Hat

Materials: one large white paper dinner napkin, approximately 15-inches square; scissors; and tape

For pilgrim hat: Place napkin on the table so it is folded in half once. Turn the unfolded decorated edge back about one-and-one-half inches and crease. Use scissors to make two two-inch long slits in the folded edge, about five inches from each end. Lap section A slightly over section C and secure with tape, forming the back of the cap. Let section B overlap the tape to form the squared-off top of the cap. Secure with tape. Use for role playing.

For nurse's cap: Make hat as above, then turn up the bottom edge of the cap about two inches. Secure with tape.

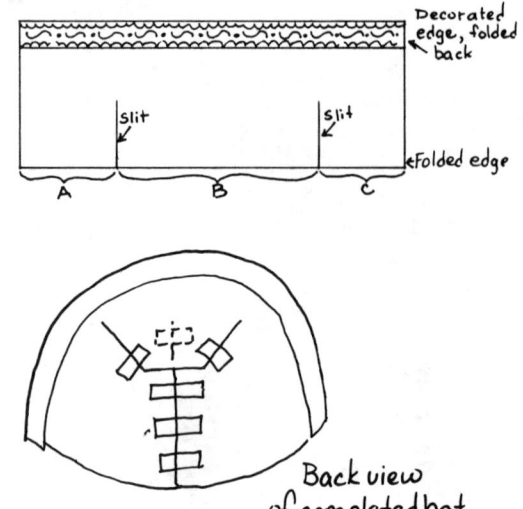

—Submitted by Nell Branum
Mount Olive, Alabama

Playing Doctor and Nurse

Materials: telephone, nurse's cap, doctor's coat, dress-up shoes, doll bed or rug for patient, stethoscope, and pictures of doctors and nurses

Sometimes doctors and nurses get a telephone call telling them of accidents or that someone is sick. They also take care of people in the hospital. Preschoolers enjoy role-playing these helpers.

—Submitted by Adele Maness
Jefferson City, Missouri

Let's Go to Church

Materials: cardboard podium; hymnals; Bible with pictures of favorite preschool Bible stories in it; and dress-up clothes and hats

Transform a corner of the room into a pretend church. Use a cardboard podium and chairs placed in rows. If a toy piano or organ is available, place it at the front. Use Bible and hymnals in the area. Preschoolers enjoy dressing up and then going to church, "preaching" their favorite Bible story, and singing songs. Small baskets may be used for the offering.

Role playing offers an excellent opportunity to help preschoolers discuss and learn more about churches.

—Submitted by Helen Posey
Vicksburg, Mississippi

Bathtime

Materials: plastic dishpan, large bath towel, baby washcloth, baby towel, small container of baby powder, receiving blanket, real baby clothes, disposable diapers, plastic smock, washable dolls, and plastic baby bottles

As preschoolers arrive in the homeliving area, let them put water into the dishpan. Place the pan on the bath towel to absorb any water that might spill. Let preschoolers take turns washing the baby.

Smocks made from plastic trash-can liners protect clothing. Slit one side from the bottom up, cut holes for head and arms. Fasten with a spring-type clothespin.

After bathing the baby, let preschoolers dress it. Suggest that only a small amount of the powder be used, since everyone will want to put powder on the baby. When the baby is powdered and dressed, preschoolers can pretend to feed it from the bottle. Be sure the preschoolers help with cleaning up the water and powder.

Talk about when the preschoolers were babies and that their mothers and daddies bathed them just as they have bathed the doll. This could provide the opportunity to talk about Baby Jesus and Mary bathing him just as they have bathed the doll. Say: Thank You, God, for babies and for mothers and daddies.

—Submitted by Carolyn Dyer
Lexington, Kentucky

Sewing on Burlap

Materials: burlap, felt-tip marker, yarn, and plastic yarn needles

Cut the burlap into 8-by-11-inch pieces. Print a child's name in manuscript letters on the burlap. Thread the needles with yarn, tying a knot in the end of the yarn. Guide the preschoolers as they follow the outline of the letters to sew their names by using a running stitch. Older fives can usually follow outlined letters. If you feel that the preschoolers cannot follow outlined letters, draw shapes on the burlap. This activity can also be adapted for fours by allowing them to simply sew on the burlap without any outline to follow.

—Submitted by Cornelia Branton Turrittin
Hampton, Virginia

Compare Fresh Orange with Mandarin

Materials: an orange, can of mandarin oranges, can opener, plate, napkins, and picture of orange trees

Open the can of mandarins and drain the sections on a plate. As you peel the orange, say: A mandarin is a type of orange. It is smaller and sweeter than this orange.
   Let the preschoolers taste the two oranges.

—Submitted by Linda Wayne
Ozark, Alabama

Sorting, Matching, Folding

Materials: pairs of socks, washcloths, small laundry basket

Lead the preschoolers to sort the laundry:
1. Put all the socks together.
2. Put all the washcloths together.
3. Match the same size, color, or design of socks.
4. Fold the washcloths and stack.

Help the preschoolers identify the users of the socks and how washcloths are used.

—Submitted by Dixie Ruth Crase
Memphis, Tennessee

Missionary Paper Dolls

Materials: figures cut from a catalog; poster board; glue; clear self-adhesive plastic; cutout outfits, such as suit, farming clothes, doctor's coat, native dress; accessories, such as shovel, Bible, stethoscope, etc.

Choose figures from a catalog to represent a missionary family. Mount the figures on poster board, and then cover with clear self-adhesive plastic for durability.

The child dresses the missionary family members as he tells or acts out the missionary's work.

—Submitted by Jane Taylor Howell
Owensboro, Kentucky

Dishes

Materials: plastic lids; colorful self-adhesive plastic; plastic knives, forks, and spoons; lids from fabric softener; and plastic scoops from soft-drink mix

Use plastic lids for plates and smaller plastic lids for saucers. Decorate the lids with colorful self-adhesive plastic. The scoops may be decorated with a narrow strip of self-adhesive plastic around the side of the cup. The fabric softener lids are for glasses. Use plastic forks, spoons, and knives to complete the place settings.

—Submitted by Dorothy Thayer Jones
Midwest City, Oklahoma

Meat-Tray Sewing Cards

Materials: Styrofoam meat trays, pictures, ballpoint pen, shoelaces, and stapler

Choose a picture that relates to the unit of study. Staple the picture onto a meat tray. Use a ballpoint pen to punch holes around the picture. Preschoolers may use a shoelace or a piece of yarn (end dipped in glue to form a point) to sew in and out of the holes.

—Submitted by Nell Branum
Mount Olive, Alabama

Container for Candy, Cookies, or Plants

Materials: one- or two-liter plastic bottle, scissors, hole punch, and pipe cleaner

Cut the bottom section of the bottle away from the rest of bottle. Punch a hole on each side of the cutout section. Fasten a pipe cleaner through the holes to form a handle across the top of the cutout section. This can be used to hold candy or cookies or as a planter.

—Submitted by Dorothy Thayer Jones
Midwest City, Oklahoma

Place Mats for Setting the Table

Materials: 11-by-17-inch waxed paper sheets; cutouts representing flatware, circles for plates, circles for glasses, and rectangles for napkins

Before the session, arrange the cutouts as a place setting on a sheet of waxed paper. Place a second sheet over this and press with a medium-hot iron to seal. Make as many place mats as there are places at the homeliving table in the room.

At the session, place the mats on the table as guides for setting the table during homeliving activities.

—Submitted by Betty Barber
Clinton, Mississippi

Sewing Cards

Materials: empty hosiery box; colorful poster board pieces (5-inch circles, squares, and triangles); colorful yarn (24-inch lengths); large bobby pins; and hole punch

Lead an older preschooler to punch holes in the set of poster board pieces. Thread each bobby pin with a piece of yarn. Suggest that the child sew the yarn in and out the holes in the poster board to create a pleasing design. The child may identify shapes of the pieces and/or describe his design. Store cards in the empty hosiery box.

Alternate

Outline a seasonal shape (pumpkin, turkey, bell, Christmas tree, flower) on the poster board. Punch holes at various points on the outline. Attach a piece of yarn long enough to complete the outline.

—Submitted by Dixie Ruth Crase
Memphis, Tennessee
and
Patti Roden
Martinez, Georgia

Skillet or Pan and Dustpan

Materials: one plastic gallon container, pen or pencil, and scissors

Outline the shape of a pan or skillet on the plastic container using a pencil or pen, as shown in diagram A. Cut out the pan or skillet with scissors and bend the cut side down to form the handle.

To make the dustpan, cut the plastic container that has a handle on one side of it. Begin at the arrow on diagram B and cut around the handle as shown to make the base of the dustpan.

—Submitted by Dorothy Thayer Jones
Midwest City, Oklahoma

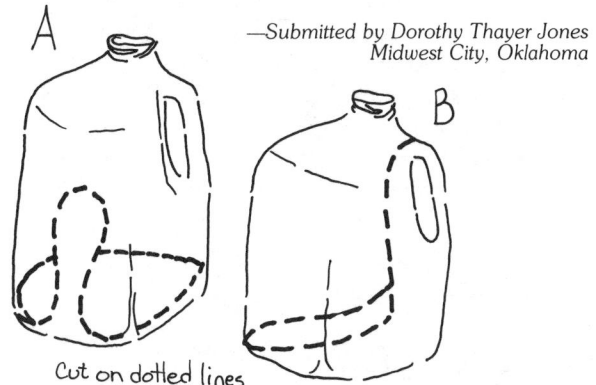

Easy-to-Dress Sunsuit for Doll

Materials: cotton fabric, scissors, sewing machine, thread, and Velcro fasteners

Cut two of the pattern. Put right sides together and sew all around except at the bottom. Turn right-side-out. Turn in at the bottom the same as other seams. Top-stitch all around. Put Velcro fasteners on neck and bottom ends. Put the sunsuit on the doll and fasten in the back.

—Submitted by Linda Wayne
Ozark, Alabama

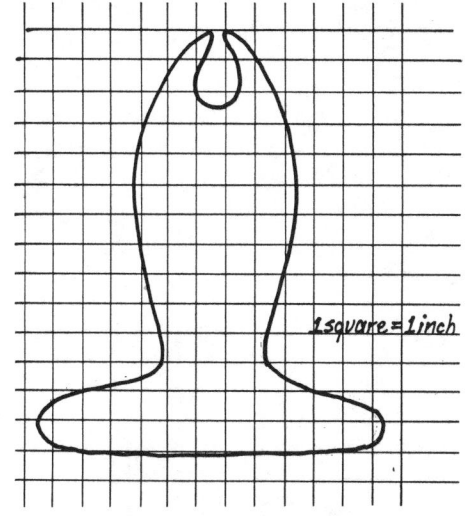

Fruit Salad

Materials: one orange, one apple, one banana, plastic knives, large bowl, spoon, small bowls, and spoons

Let the preschoolers take turns cutting the fruit into small pieces in the large bowl. Stir lightly with a spoon. Serve in small bowls.

—Submitted by Margie A. Black
Cartersville, Georgia

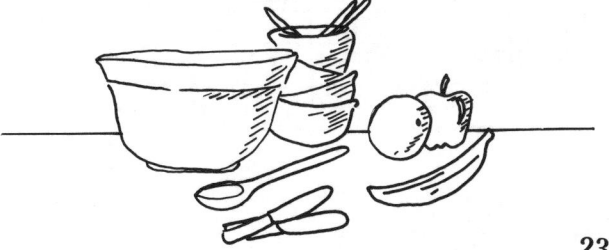

Mailbox

Materials: shoe box, scissors, masking tape, three brads, yarn, red poster board, and solid-color self-adhesive plastic

Cut two corners at the end of an open shoe box to make an opening. Leave the bottom seam attached. Open the flap. Tape on the top of the shoe box. If desired, cover the box and flap with solid-color self-adhesive plastic. Cut a mailbox flag from red poster board. Put a brad through the mailbox flag and the right side of the mailbox. Insert one brad in the top of the box at the open end and one in the flap. Tie a five-inch piece of yarn to the brad on the flap. To close the mailbox, wrap the yarn around the brad on the box top.

Preschoolers may use the box in dramatic play, such as for mailing letters to and receiving letters from missionaries and others.

—Submitted by Cornelia Branton Turritin
Hampton, Virginia

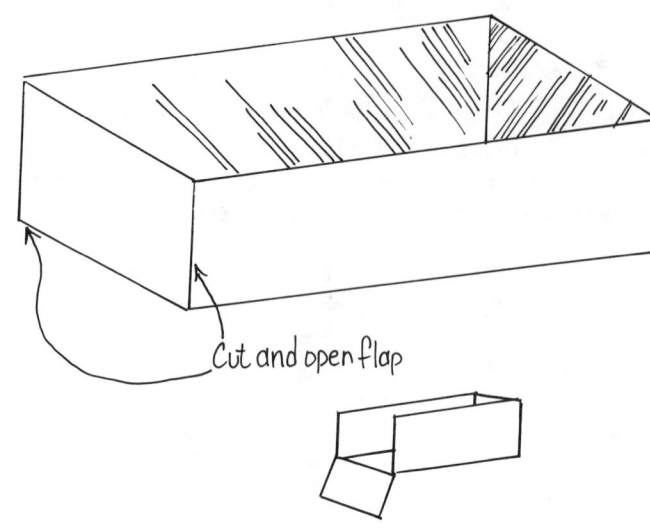

Needlepoint

Materials: plastic fruit or vegetable basket, white glue, yarn (approximately 20 inches long), and scissors

Cut the sides from the basket. Dip one end of the yarn in glue to make a point. Tie the yarn to a corner of the bottom. Weave the yarn in and out of the plastic to make designs. Two or three different colors of yarn can be used with older preschoolers.

—Submitted by Johanna Dawson
Albuquerque, New Mexico

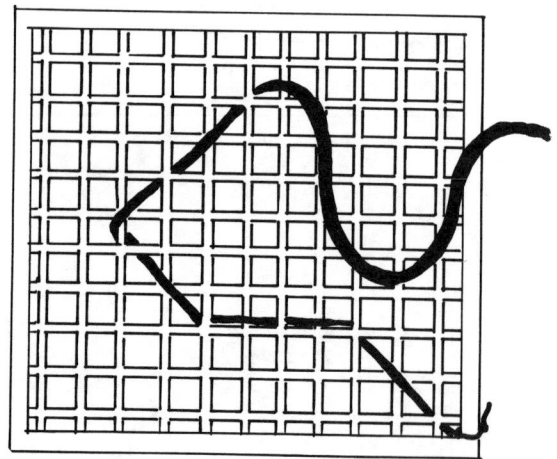

Multiuse Homeliving Toy

Materials: plastic dishpan, preferably with hole for hanging; clear self-adhesive plastic, same size as bottom of dishpan; one piece of black construction paper; and one heavy-duty shoelace

Convert the plastic dishpan into a stove top by cutting four electric coils out of the black construction paper. Glue them to the underneath side of the dishpan and cover with clear self-adhesive plastic.

After preschoolers cook their meal, they can turn the dishpan over and wash and store the dishes. The same dishpan, or another, can be used as a doll bed.

String a sturdy shoelace through the hanging hole to make a toddler pull-toy.

This toy is useful for programs with tight budgets or in rooms which must be shared with other age groups and is easily removed for storage.

—Submitted by Eloise Stinchcomb
Randallstown, Maryland

Brads
Use a 5" piece of yarn to close.

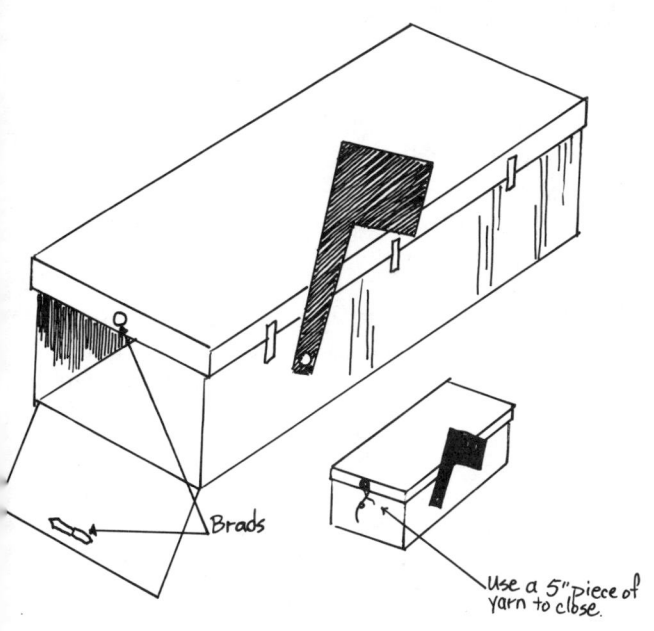

Shopping at the Grocery Store

Materials: cash register; toy money; grocery bags or boxes; toy shopping cart, empty food boxes and cans; and plastic fruit and vegetables

When emptying a can to use at home, open the bottom of the can. This makes the can appear unopened when turned right-side-up. Place items in the homeliving area to stimulate role playing of shoppers and grocery store employees.

—Submitted by Sharon B. Garnett
Chesapeake, Virginia

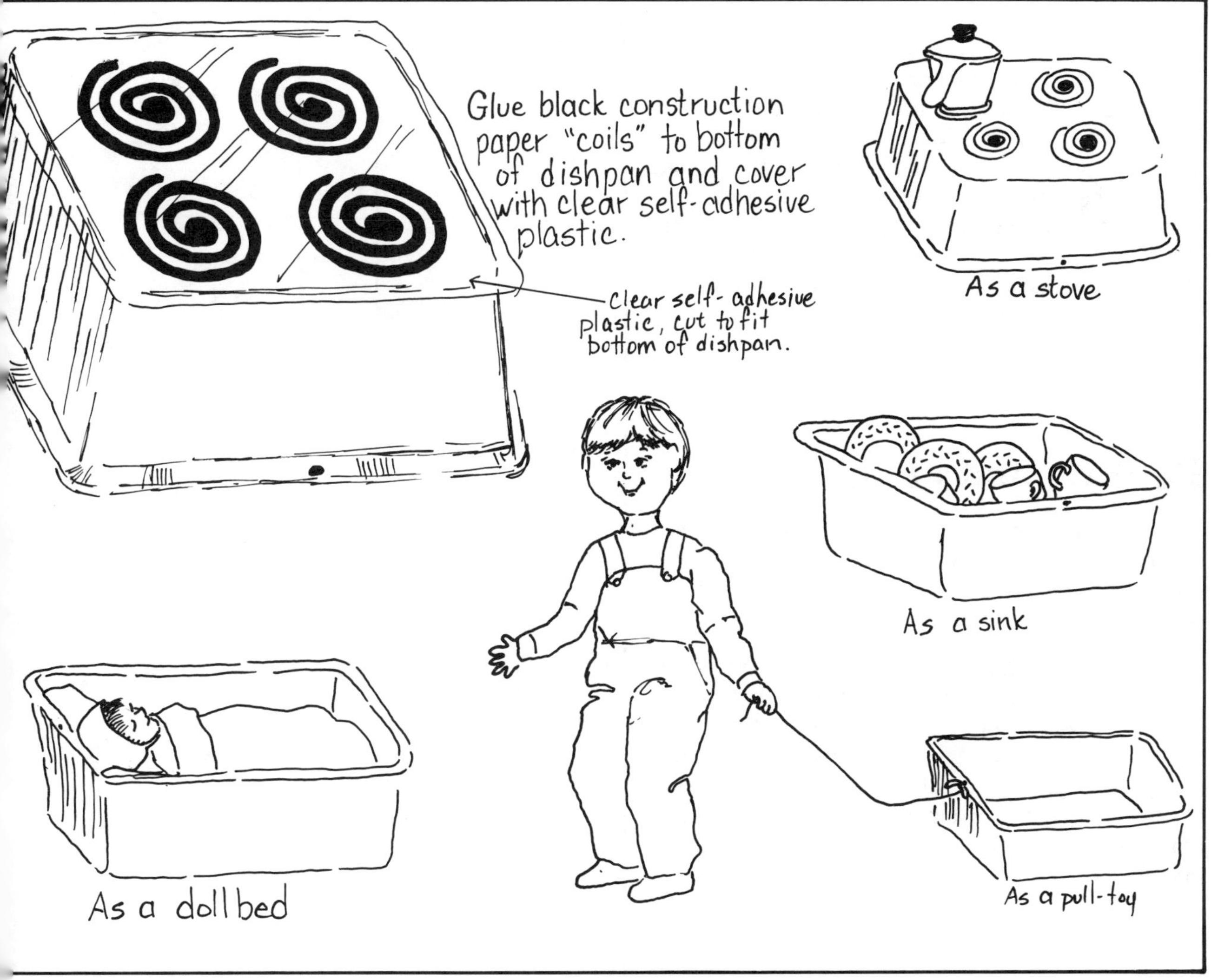

Glue black construction paper "coils" to bottom of dishpan and cover with clear self-adhesive plastic.
Clear self-adhesive plastic, cut to fit bottom of dishpan.
As a stove
As a sink
As a doll bed
As a pull-toy

Painted Cookies

Materials: sugar cookies, confectioners sugar, milk, vanilla, food coloring, small containers, sterilized watercolor paintbrushes, spoons, and napkins

Mix small amounts of milk with powdered sugar and food coloring in the small containers. First, the preschoolers wash hands. Then let them paint designs on the cookies placed on napkins. These cookies may be used as a gift.

—Submitted by Nina Edwards
Mustang, Oklahoma

Window Poster

Materials: one sheet white poster board; one strip of colorful fabric, 45-by-6 inches; scenic nature poster of mountains, snow, or beach; double-stick cellophane tape; and clear self-adhesive plastic

Measure and cut the poster board into the shape of a window frame. Cover the window with clear self-adhesive plastic. Hem the edges of the fabric and gather the top edge to fit the width of the window. Staple or glue the curtain to the upper edge of the window. Attach a scenic poster to the back of the window with double-stick tape. Hang the window in the homeliving area to promote discussion. The poster may be changed according to the unit of study.

—Submitted by Sue M. Perry
Gulfport, Mississippi

Pouring and Measuring

Materials: a variety of dried beans (pintos, black-eyed peas, navy beans, black beans, lima beans); large box; measuring cups; funnels; wooden spoons; and an old sheet

Place the dried beans in the box. Spread the sheet on the floor and put the box in the middle of the sheet. Older preschoolers enjoy pouring, stirring, measuring, and manipulating the beans. They can discover how many small cups it takes to fill the larger cups, etc. For cleanup time, pick up the corners of the sheet and dump the beans back into the box.

—Submitted by Gayle Lintz
Waco, Texas

Dress Closet

Materials: a wardrobe box; utility knife; tape; dress-up clothes; and hangers

Obtain a wardrobe box from a moving company. The box has a removable bar across the center for hanging clothes. Cut the box to child-size, leaving flaps to close the top. Cut new bar holders and tape the bar in place.

This is a prop for dramatic play and an organizer for the homeliving area. Gather outgrown clothes from nine- or ten-year-olds for the preschoolers to use.

—Submitted by Carolyn F. Singleton
Summerville, South Carolina

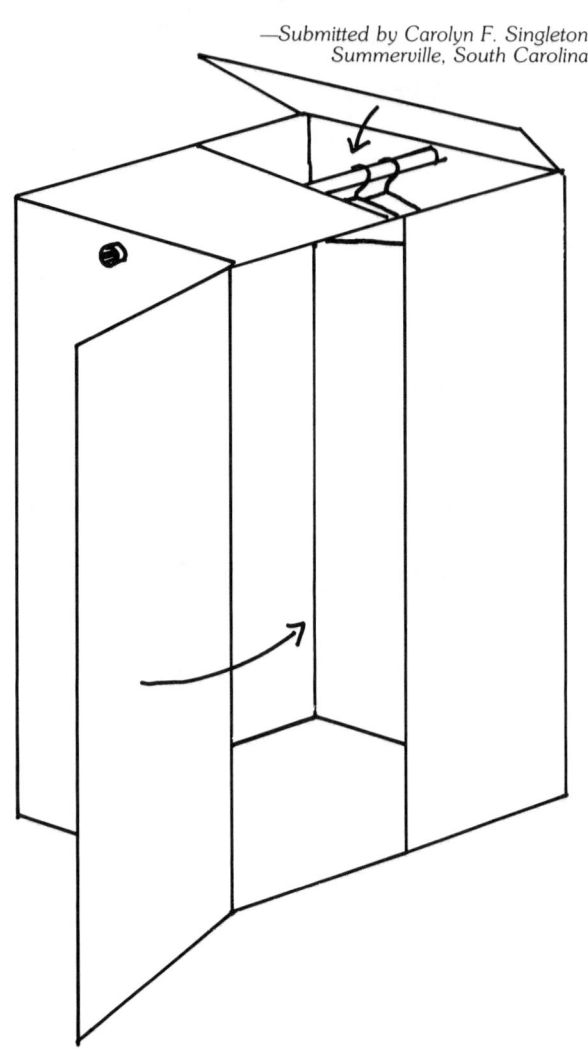

Nature

"Show me what God made."

Fun in the Wind

Materials: colored crepe paper

Cut strips of crepe paper into three-foot lengths. Take preschoolers outside on a windy day. Tie a strip of crepe paper around each child's wrist. Let the child hold it up for the wind to blow it, or run with it streaming behind him. Good exercise!

This activity presents an opportunity to talk about wind as air moving and how God provides it. Say: Winds blow the clouds through the sky. Wind scatters seeds from flowers and trees. The wind feels cool on our faces. God sends the wind.

—*Submitted by Leona Olin Tucker
Kenton, Oklahoma*

Fruits, Vegetables, and Their Seeds

Materials: fruits; vegetables; magazine or catalog pictures of fruits and vegetables; small paper plates; glue; scissors; construction paper; plastic knife; five-by-seven-inch pieces of poster board; and clear self-adhesive plastic

Mount pictures of fruits or vegetables to be displayed on poster boards. Cover each board with clear self-adhesive plastic for durability. Place a variety of fruits and vegetables and the matching poster boards in the nature area.

Talk with the boys and girls about the fruits and vegetables. Let them feel each item. Say: How does the apple feel? Is it rough or smooth? God provides good food for us to eat, and we thank God for the food.

Cut the fruits and vegetables into small sections for preschoolers to taste. Remove the seeds, and place them in the paper plates.

Lead each child to choose a seed to paste on a piece of construction paper. Suggest that he pick out the fruit or vegetable that belongs to the seed.

Talk about:
- When a seed is planted and cared for properly, it makes a new plant of the same kind.
- Some foods are eaten raw, cooked, or dried.
- We eat different parts of foods: leaves (lettuce), roots (carrots), flowers or stems (broccoli).
- Sometimes we eat the skins of fruit (apples, pears, cherries, figs, dates); some skins we do not eat (bananas, grapefruit, oranges).

—Submitted by Carolyn Dyer
Lexington, Kentucky
and
Renva Acree
Blairsville, Georgia

Experiences with a Coconut

Materials: hammer, grater, knife, paper cups, screwdriver or ice pick, and bowl

Place a screwdriver or ice pick over the "eyes" of a coconut, one at a time, and hammer it through the shell. Drain the milk into the paper cups for the preschoolers to taste. Split the coconut and peel it. Lead the preschoolers to help grate the coconut into the bowl, then taste it.

Tell them that coconuts grow on coconut palm trees in places where it is warm all the time. Besides the coconut meat that they have eaten, a valuable oil or fat comes from the coconut. This is used to make soap, margarine, and some other food items, such as cereals. The husk of the coconut seed, which is removed before the coconuts are sold, is full of thread-like fibers that people use to make ropes, brooms, and mats.

—Submitted by Jackie Rodgers
Bedford, Texas

Observing Bean Seeds

Materials: egg carton, 12 egg shell halves, potting soil, and bean seeds

Lead the preschoolers to place the egg shells in the egg carton. Suggest that they fill each shell with potting soil. Lead them to push a finger gently into the soil of each shell to make a hole. Suggest that they put two or three seeds in each hole and gently cover the seed with dirt. Lead the child to water each one carefully. Place the carton in a sunny window. Every day dig up the seeds in one of the shells. Show the preschooler the interesting changes that happen to seeds underground. Keep digging up seeds each day until you have only two or three shells left. Tap these shells gently on the bottom to crack them. Plant the bean seedlings, egg shells and all, into a garden or large pots.

—Submitted by Gayle Lintz
Waco, Texas

Place seedlings in garden or large pots.

Observing Gourds

Materials: fresh gourds (if available); dried, whole gourds with loose seeds still inside; dried gourds cut in half for dippers; dried gourds made into bird houses

Lead the preschoolers to handle the gourds. Discuss the different shapes, sizes, textures, and uses. Have water available for preschoolers to dip with the halved gourds. Lead preschoolers to shake the whole gourds with loose seeds. Play a recording and let them keep time to the music.

—Submitted by Eloise Stinchcomb
Randallstown, Maryland

Identify Smells

Materials: plastic medicine bottles from drugstore; cotton balls; and various spices, seasonings, and foods (lemon, onion, chocolate, tea, coffee)

Put different spices, seasonings, and foods on cotton balls, and place the balls inside the medicine bottles.
 Let the preschoolers close their eyes and sniff lightly at each bottle to try to identify the scent.

—Submitted by Mrs. Fred Halbrooks
Louisville, Kentucky

Backpacking

Materials: medium-size grocery sack for each child; 18-inch pieces of yarn (two per child); crayons; felt-tip markers; stickers; pictures; paste; food (could be a snack made in homeliving); and paper cups

Reinforce the sack by turning down a two-inch rim around the top. Punch holes and make yarn loops for arms. Lead the preschoolers to use crayons and other art materials to decorate their sacks. Invite each child to pack his backpack with a snack, a paper cup, and maybe a towel rolled up for a sleeping bag. Suggest that preschoolers wear their backpacks on a nature hike. Find a spot where preschoolers can spread the "sleeping bags" and enjoy the snack from their backpacks. Serve water or juice from a thermos. Watch for birds and changes in the sky. Listen to outdoor sounds.

Easy Watering Cups

Materials: aerosol spray-can caps small enough to hold the amount of water needed for seeds planted in paper cups

Following a seed-planting activity, give the preschooler a cap from an aerosol can just the right size to hold the amount of water needed each day to make the seed grow. Instruct the child to put just that amount of water on the seed each day, no more or no less. This helps the child to learn how to help plants to grow.

—Submitted by Betty Backer
Clinton, Mississippi

Bug Bottle

Materials: clear, plastic detergent or milk bottle; a light-colored nylon stocking; insect or other nature item; and knife or scissors

Use a detergent bottle with at least two flat sides. With a knife or scissors, cut a large hole in each side of the bottle. Place the insect or nature item in the bottle and quickly pull the hose over the bottle, stretching the hose tightly. Tie a knot at each end of the stocking. This is one of the safest ways to view insects.

—Submitted by Susan Hardison
Washington, Vermont

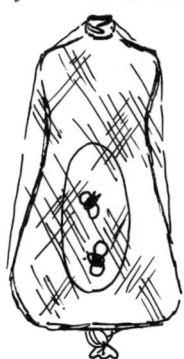

Find Out About Air

Materials: musical instruments that must be blown to produce sound (clarinets, French horns, oboes); balloons; paper bag; drinking straws; pinwheel; bubble soap; candle; glass; paper; water; and large bowl or dishpan

Preschoolers are not aware of the air around them or the importance of air in our world. Help them become aware of some of the following concepts:
- Air is necessary and is everywhere.
- Air moves. Observe smoke, clouds, windmills, kites, trees, seeds, and sailboats.
- Air cannot be seen, smelled, or tasted, but can be felt when it moves.

Use the following experiments with the preschoolers:
- Blow into musical instruments to show how air produces sound.
- Inflate a balloon to show pressure. Blow soap bubbles.
- Inflate and pop a paper bag. Drink through a straw.
- Blow against a pinwheel and watch it turn.
- Light a candle and place an inverted glass over it. When the air in the glass is used up, the candle will go out. Fire must have air.
- Light a candle and place a glass in front of it. Blow on the glass and watch the candle go out as the air moves around the glass.
- Place a wadded-up piece of paper in the bottom of a drinking glass. Fill a large bowl or dishpan about half full with water. Turn the glass upside down, keep it level, and push it down quickly into the water. (Do not tilt glass.) Lift the glass out of the water carefully, still keeping it level. Notice that the wad of paper is dry. Discuss that the air in the glass kept the paper dry. Lower the glass into the water again. Tilt it to let the preschoolers watch the air escape as they see the bubbles.

As preschoolers experiment with air, use the Bible thought, Think of the wonders of God (see Job 37:14).

—Submitted by Christine McCauley
Tallahassee, Florida

Whose House Is This?

Materials: magnetic photo album with ten pages, pictures of animals and their homes or children of other lands and their homes or native dress

Cut the album pages in half. Place an animal or child on the top half of each page. On the bottom half, place the animal's or child's home (or native dress for child).

As the child is ready, ask questions:
Is the home made by man or by God?
What did God give man to help him build it?

If native dress is matched, the game becomes, Who Wears This?

—Submitted by Nina Edwards
Mustang, Oklahoma

Whose Home Is This?

Materials: pictures of animals, birds, and children; pictures of homes for each of these; magnetic tape; glue; and poster board

Examples of pictures are: barn and horse; house and children; spiderweb and spider; pond and frog; and nest and bird.

Place the pictures of different kinds of homes that either God or man has provided on poster board. At the bottom of each mounted picture, put a small strip of magnetic tape. Mount the pictures of animals and children on other posterboard cards. Place a small strip of magnetic tape on the back of each of these cards.

Suggest that the preschoolers match each animal with the home provided for it. Ask: Did God or man make this home? Did God help the animal know how to make its own home?

—Submitted by Dorothy Thayer Jones
Midwest City, Oklahoma

Nature-in-a-Book

Materials: three clear plastic container lids the same size; three slightly smaller lids; dried flowers; butterflies; pictures of nature items; hole punch; large notebook ring; and glue

Put a nature item or picture on a larger lid. Cover with a smaller lid and glue together at the edges. Punch holes in the lids. Fasten the lids together with a notebook ring to make a book. Lead preschoolers to look at the objects. Talk about all of the beautiful things God has given us to enjoy.

—Submitted by Lillian Hill
Waco, Texas

God Planned for Me Through Plants and Animals

Materials: pictures of animals (cow, chicken); pictures of plants (corn, potato, carrot, turnip, apple tree, banana plant); pictures of products from the plants and animals; poster board; glue; and scissors

Cut poster board into 9-by-12-inch pieces. Glue on pictures of the plants and animals. Glue the food which that plant or animal produces on 4-by-4-inch pieces of poster board. Preschoolers match the plant or animal with its product(s). Examples are: cow—milk; chicken—eggs; corn plant—corn on the cob; apple tree—apples; banana plant—bananas; potato plant—potatoes; turnip plant—turnips and greens; carrot plant—carrots.

—Submitted by Nina Edwards
Mustang, Oklahoma

Seed Book

Materials: poster board, seeds, pictures of produce, small self-sealing plastic bags, hole punch, yarn or metal ring fastener, and glue

Cut poster board into eight-by-ten-inch pieces. On each piece, paste a picture of a familiar food that grows from seeds (check seed catalogs for pictures). Below the picture attach a small plastic bag with the seed from that fruit or vegetable enclosed. Fasten pieces of poster board together with yarn or a ring fastener.

Lead the preschoolers to look at the picture and then see the seeds which when planted will produce this food they see in the picture. Lead the preschooler to feel the seeds and notice the differences in size, shape, and texture.

—Submitted by Lynda Mills
Pasadena, Texas

Feeding Birds on a String

Materials: plastic yarn needles, yarn, O-shaped cereal, and small scraps of paper

Thread the yarn through the needle. Tie a knot in the end of the yarn. Run the needle through a small piece of paper and push the paper all the way to the knot. Lead the preschooler to put the needle through the hole in each piece of cereal and thread it onto the yarn. Suggest that he continue to string the cereal until he has a long string. Help him hang the yarn on a bush outside so the birds will find it. If possible, allow the child to watch from a window as the birds eat the cereal.

Alternate: Cranberries and popcorn are other edibles to string for the birds.

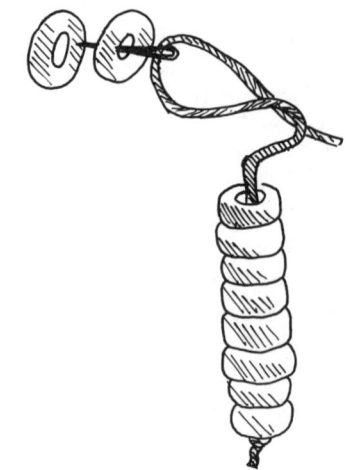

—Submitted by Connie Markham
Montpelier, Vermont

Matching Game: Seeds

Materials: seeds, plastic wrap, clear tape, and three-by-five-inch index cards

Save the seeds from different kinds of fruits and vegetables (orange, apple, grape, peach, pear, cherry, bean, etc.). Allow seeds to dry. Cut pieces of plastic wrap three inches square. Place three or four seeds of the same kind on each plastic square and fold into a one-inch square. Tape so that seeds will be secure. Fasten the square to a three-by-five-inch index card. Make two identical cards for each kind of seed.

Play a matching game with the cards. Lead the child to choose a seed card. Suggest that he find another card just like the one he has. Say: When we put these seeds in the ground, (carrots) will grow for us to eat.

—Submitted by Christine Hackler
Loveland, Ohio

A Bottle's Eye View

Materials: empty, two-liter plastic drink bottle; water; alcohol; leaves; flowers; and shells

Wash out the drink bottle. Use alcohol to remove the label and glue. Fill the bottle with water and add nature items. Replace the lid, and glue it on tightly. Allow time for the glue to dry before using.

Suggest that the preschoolers shake the bottle and observe the items in the water. The bubble action in the water may elicit discussion on air and water both being from God.

—Submitted by Penny Murphy
Bowling Green, Kentucky
and
Carolyn Sue Manley
Grand Prairie, Texas

Worms Are Useful

Materials: earthworms in a large glass jar with soil, magnifying glass, newspaper, and picture of mother bird feeding little ones (optional)

Cover the table with paper. Pour the container of worms on the paper. Preschoolers may pick up the worms. Lead the boys and girls to use a magnifying glass to watch the worms make holes in soil. Ask: Who made the worms? (God) What are they good for? (They are food for birds and fish. Worms make holes in the soil and help make the soil richer to help vegetable gardens grow. Worms are useful.)

—Submitted by Mrs. Katherine Hooks
Bowling Green, Kentucky

Artificial Snow

Materials: liquid starch or a mixture of equal parts of water and white glue; brushes; nature items (branches of pine or cedar) or blue construction paper; one-half cup granulated sugar or Epsom salts; and one-half cup flour or talcum powder

Brush liquid starch or the glue mixture over a nature item you wish to decorate. Mix sugar (or Epsom salts) with the flour (or talcum powder). Sprinkle this mixture over the wet area. Let dry. The more sugar or salts, the more sparkle.

Lead the preschooler to draw a picture on construction paper. He then brushes liquid starch or the glue mixture over the picture and sprinkles on the sugar or Epsom salts mixture. Allow the picture to dry. The picture will sparkle like snow.

—Submitted by Lou Crussel
Mustang, Oklahoma

Ocean in a Bottle

Materials: clear plastic bottle, glue, water, cooking oil, and blue or green food coloring

Fill the bottle half full of water. Then fill the bottle to the top with cooking oil (use equal parts). Leave no air in the bottle. Add a few drops of blue or green food coloring, if desired. Seal the lid tightly with permanent glue. Lead the preschooler to turn the bottle on its side and tilt it back and forth. The contents will resemble ocean waves. Talk about God's beautiful world.

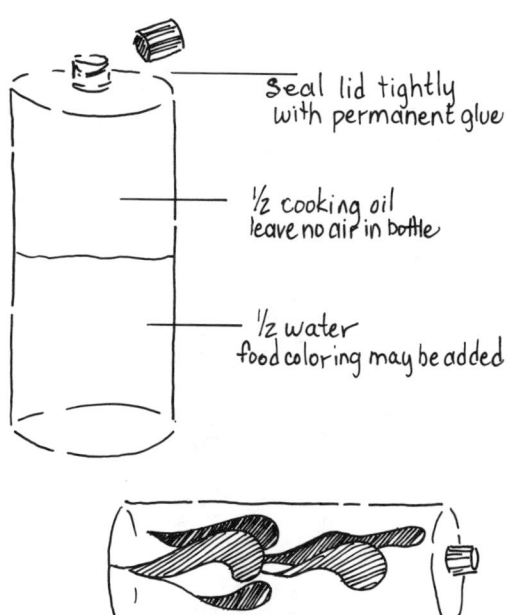

Animal Tracks

Materials: play dough; waxed paper; small amount of water; and old, large, unusually-shaped buttons

Place a few drops of water on the table to help hold down a 12-by-15-inch piece of waxed paper for each child. Place the buttons in the center of the table so each child can reach them. Divide the play dough equally among the preschoolers. Guide the preschoolers to select a button and to press it into the flattened dough. Lead them to observe the tracks the buttons leave.

Provide an encyclopedia or other books showing different kinds of animal tracks. This is for older preschoolers only. It requires close supervision to be certain the buttons are used correctly, rather than in the mouth, nose, or ears.

—Submitted by Barbara Maxwell
Kansas City, Missouri

Discovering a Rainbow

Materials: large sheet of white butcher paper, 24 inches long; and glass of water

Place the large sheet of butcher paper on the floor beneath a window. Place the glass of water on the window ledge in bright sunlight. Move the butcher paper, if necessary, to pick up the rainbow reflection from the glass of water.

Talk about what makes a rainbow. Talk about when and where we have seen a rainbow.

A Trip to the Farm

Enlist parents to help with a trip to a farm. They may assist with transportation as well as guiding the preschoolers on the tour.

Let the preschoolers walk in the pasture. Take them into the barn. Show them the animals. Arrange for them to watch the animals being fed, perhaps a young one nursing. Let them see how a cow is milked (by hand, if possible, and also by machine).

Find a grassy spot to sit down and thank God for all He has given us.

—Submitted by Martha Kate Phillips
Calhoun City, Mississippi
and
Nelda Barnes
Siloam Springs, Arkansas

Nature Album

Materials: medium-size magnetic picture album and various sizes of pictures of nature objects

Place the pictures torn from magazines on a table with the album. Lead older preschoolers to choose pictures to cut out. Suggest that they place the picture on a page of the album, and smooth the plastic sheet in place. Preschoolers might add pictures to the album each session until it is filled. Print appropriate Bible thoughts on each page. Place the album on the bookshelf or in the nature area.

—Submitted by Leona Olin Tucker
Kenton, Oklahoma

Tasting Pineapple

Materials: pineapple, knife, cutting board, cups, and plastic knives

Talk with the preschoolers about God making fruit. Lead the preschoolers to smell the pineapple and hold it in their hands. Cut the pineapple in half from top to bottom. Remove the core. Give preschoolers plastic knives to cut the pineapple into little pieces for a snack. Give each child a paper cup in which to put pineapple pieces.

—Submitted by Jackie Rodgers
Bedford, Texas

Identify Sounds

Materials: cassette recorder, blank cassette tapes, and sounds

Record sounds on a cassette tape.
Church Sounds: organ, piano, choir, money in offering plate, church bell, footsteps, turning pages in a Bible
Home Sounds: water running, food cooking, telephone, doorbell, baby crying, children playing, ball bouncing, dog barking, cat crying, wind blowing leaves, water lapping on shore, piano
Around Town Sounds: car horn, train, airplane, traffic, cash register
Lead the preschooler to listen to the tape and identify the sounds.

—Submitted by Martha Harless
Enid, Oklahoma
and
Deena Williams Newman
Birmingham, Alabama

Nature Walk

Take preschoolers for a walk outdoors any season of the year. Lead them to look around and tell what they see. Suggest that they listen with their eyes closed, then open, and tell what they hear.

Sit outside in a covered area and watch a thunderstorm approaching. Encourage the child to listen to the distant thunder, to look at the faint light from lightning, and to smell the air as the storm comes closer.

Lead the preschoolers to walk in the rain, if they are properly dressed, to feel the drops, to watch them as they splash on leaves and form puddles.
Note: Never take preschoolers walking in the rain when there is lightning.

—Submitted by Jennifer Cox
Birmingham, Alabama
and
Kay Westbrook
Chattanooga, Tennessee

Sunny/Rainy Reversible Pictures

Materials: one paper plate and one tongue depressor or craft stick for each child; crayons; and paste

Lead the preschooler to draw a picture of a sunny day on one side of his paper plate. Suggest that he draw a rainy day on the other side of the plate. Guide the child to use paste to mount the plate on a tongue depressor or craft stick for a handle.

Sing together "It's a Pretty Day," page 78, *Music for Today's Children*.[1] Lead preschoolers to hold up the appropriate side of their paper plates as they sing *It's a sunny day* and *It's a rainy day*.

[1]Available through Baptist Book Stores.

—Submitted by Nell Branum
Mount Olive, Alabama

Sounds

Materials: an even number of 35-millimeter film containers, sand, paper clips, gravel, acorns, beads, and other small household items

Place sand in two containers, paper clips in two containers, gravel in two containers, and so on to make matching sets of sounds. Securely seal the containers with glue and/or tape. Place the containers on the nature shelf. Suggest that the preschooler choose a container, shake it to hear the sound, then shake the other containers until he finds the one that matches the sound of the one he chose.

—Submitted by Mrs. Fred Halbrooks
Louisville, Kentucky

Colored Bubbles

Materials: one cup soap powder, one quart warm water, drinking straws, a few drops of food coloring (optional), and small cans or cups

Mix the soap in the water to dissolve. Add food coloring, and mix well. Provide each child with a straw and some of the mixture in a small can or cup. Lead the boys and girls to blow through the straw into the soap mixture to create colored bubbles.

Talk about air being inside each bubble. When the bubble bursts, air is realeased. State that air is everywhere.

—Submitted by Kaylene Richardson
Louisville, Kentucky

Animal Homes-Sorting Game

Materials: pictures of animals which live in water, on land, and in the air; and three sacks—one with a picture of a pond, one with the sky, and one with a picture of land

Tell the preschoolers to sort the animal pictures according to the place the animals live. They will place the pictures in the appropriate sack. (Variation: animals that live on the farm, in the forest, in the jungle.)

—Submitted by Patti Roden
Martinez, Georgia

Object Match

Materials: seasonal nature objects too large to swallow; poster board; felt-tip marker; and clear self-adhesive plastic

Outline the nature objects with the felt-tip marker on the poster board and cover with clear self-adhesive plastic.

Place the board on the floor with the nature items around the edges. Guide the preschoolers to handle and examine the items. Help them identify the items. Ask: What is this? What did it come from? How is it used?

Lead the preschoolers to match the item to the outline on the board. Encourage them to take turns handling and matching the items.

—Submitted by Kaye Riggs
Houston, Texas

A Nature Frieze

Materials: a long piece of butcher paper; tempera paint; paintbrushes; fasteners; and paint smocks

Fasten the paper to a wall or place it on a smooth floor. Divide paper into three sections vertically. Print *Things in the Sky* on one section. Print *Things on Land* on another section, and *Things Underground or in the Water* on the last section.

Each child wears a paint smock. Lead preschoolers to paint the blue sky in section one. Then in the middle section, preschoolers paint green grass as well as the blue sky. The third section has lots of brown soil and some blue water over to one side.

With the backgrounds completed, the preschoolers either paste pictures cut from magazines in the appropriate section, or draw an object or animal to paste on the frieze.

—*Submitted by Adele Maness*
Jefferson City, Missouri

Showing Slides

Materials: slide projector with remote control; one or more slide sets with subject areas related to the unit, such as animal mothers and babies, farm animals, zoo animals, different churches, community helpers, plants, etc.; a large box (approximately 24 inches square); and white paper or white sheet to line the bottom of the box

Cover the inside bottom of the box with the white paper or sheet. Arrange the slides in the carousel to place in the projector. Turn the box on its side. Project the slides on the bottom of the box.

Talk to the preschoolers about what they see on each slide. Make applications to the unit.

—*Submitted by Zadabeth Uland*
Plano, Texas

Puzzles

"I can put it together."

Tube and Spool Puzzle

Materials: paper-towel tube/and several spools of assorted sizes

Younger preschoolers will enjoy placing spools inside the paper-towel tube. When the tube is removed carefully, a preschooler is delighted to find a free-standing stack of spools.

—Submitted by Nell Branum
Mount Olive, Alabama

Key Match

Materials: old keys in different sizes and shapes, poster board or manila file folder, and an envelope to hold the keys

Trace around the keys on the inside of a file folder or on the poster board. Attach the envelope to the outside of the file folder or back of the poster board. The preschoolers match the keys to their outlines.

—Submitted by Betty Barber
Clinton, Mississippi

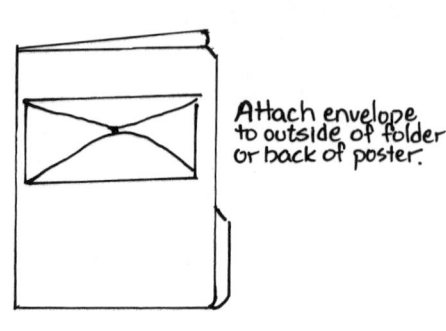

Outline keys.

Attach envelope to outside of folder or back of poster.

Feel and Match

Materials: a closed cardboard box; two each of an assortment of familiar objects; and two box lids

In the cardboard box, cut a hole just large enough for a child's hand to slip through. Place one of each of the paired objects in the box and close it. Place the matching object on one of the box lids.

To play, the child chooses an object from the lid, feels it, and then places it in the other lid. He reaches into the closed box and feels for the matching item. When he finds it, he brings it out of the box and places it with its mate on the box lid. Another child takes a turn, or the same child continues to match other objects.

For variety, do not provide the items to be matched. Allow a preschooler to feel an object, guess what it is, and then remove the object to see if the guess was correct.

Older preschoolers may sort the items into two groups: hard and soft.

—Submitted by Renva Acree
Blairsville, Georgia

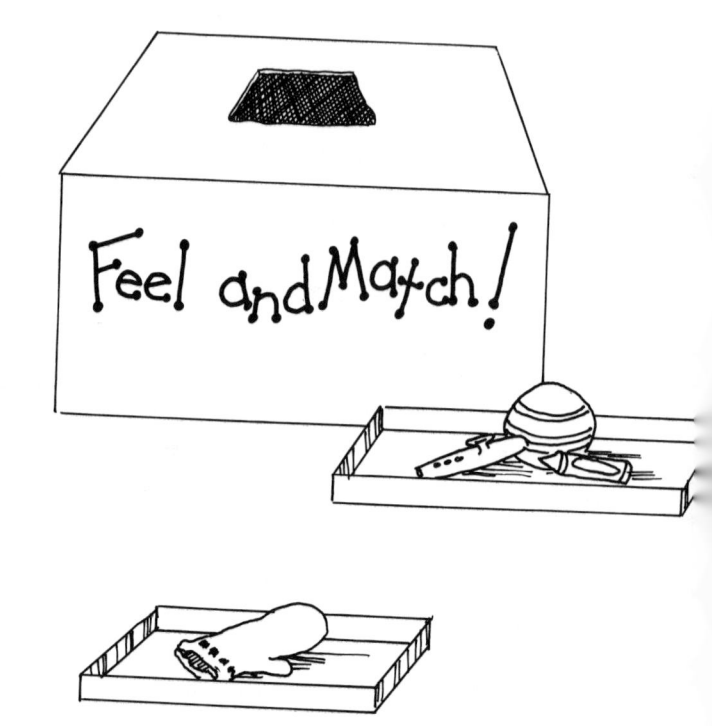

Paper-Plate Puzzles

Materials: paper plates, magazine or resource kit pictures, glue, clear self-adhesive plastic, and scissors

Cut each picture in a circle to fit a paper plate. Glue the picture onto the plate and allow to dry. Cover the picture on the plate with clear self-adhesive plastic for durability. Cut the plate in six or eight pie-shaped pieces. Place each puzzle in a large envelope for storage. This is an inexpensive way to make puzzles.

—Submitted by Carol Miller Kay
Calhoun City, Mississippi

Cover with clear self adhesive plastic before cutting.

Cookie-Sheet Puzzle

Materials: steel cookie sheet, magnetic tape, teaching pictures, poster board, scissors, and rubber cement

Put a picture on poster board with the rubber cement. Carefully smooth out any wrinkles. Cut the puzzle into easy-to-handle pieces. Glue a small piece of magnetic tape to the back of each piece. Preschoolers assemble the puzzle on the cookie sheet.

—Submitted by Neva Starnes
Delta Junction, Alaska

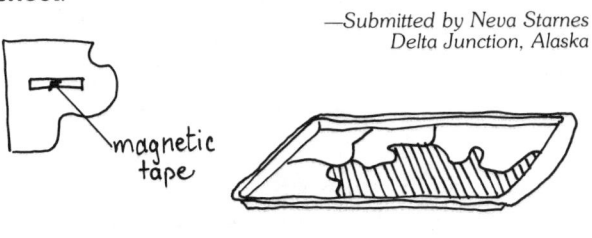

magnetic tape

Objects Puzzle

Materials: large gift box; collection of small objects found in the home, such as plastic spoon, bottle cap, key, or comb; and felt-tip marker

On the inside of the box lid, trace the shape of each object collected. Place that object in the box bottom. During the session encourage the boys and girls to fit each object on its place. The game may be stored by putting objects in the box bottom and closing the top.

A variation of this puzzle could be a puzzle for learning to set the table. For older preschoolers, use a plastic knife, fork, spoon, small unbreakable plate, paper cup, and napkin. Trace objects in the proper place for setting the table. Younger preschoolers could use a spoon, dish or bowl, cup, and napkin and follow the same directions.

—Submitted by Renva Acree
Blairsville, Georgia

Puzzle in a File Folder: "God Gives Food"

Materials: manila file folder; pictures of cow, milk products, chicken, eggs, trees, fruits, grain growing, and bread; clear self-adhesive plastic; construction paper; glue; envelope; and scissors

Cut a sheet of construction paper to fit the inside of the file folder. Glue pictures of foods to the paper. Glue the paper inside the folder. Cover the paper with clear self-adhesive plastic for durability. Glue pictures of the sources of these foods to squares of construction paper. Cover the squares with clear self-adhesive plastic. Tape an envelope to the back of the folder to store the puzzle pieces. When the session is over, place the puzzle in a picture file box or resource kit file.

—Submitted by Lillian Hill
Waco, Texas

Flower Puzzles

Materials: pictures of flowers from a seed catalog, cardboard, glue, and scissors

Mount the pictures on cardboard. Cut the pictures into two or three pieces, according to the age of the preschoolers. The young ones enjoy matching the pieces.

—Submitted by Martha Harless
Enid, Oklahoma

Make a Picture

Materials: felt squares of assorted colors, scissors, and self-sealing plastic bag or envelope for storage

The teacher cuts various shapes from the felt pieces (squares, circles, rectangles, ovals, triangles, strips, etc.) in several colors. Encourage the preschoolers to make pictures from the felt shapes on felt squares. This may be used as a table, floor, or wall puzzle.

—Submitted by Margaret E. Pennington
Tucson, Arizona

Match the Pictures

Materials: two matching pictures, construction paper, glue, and scissors

Glue two matching pictures onto construction paper, choosing a different color on which to mount each picture. Cut one picture into about six pieces. Lead the preschooler to work the puzzle to match the whole picture.

—Submitted by Sue Brown
Louisville, Kentucky

Puzzle Book

Materials: spiral or three-ring notebook, full-page pictures, construction paper, scissors, and glue

This puzzle book will contain some large pictures appropriate for preschoolers. In between each picture is a blank page cut into three or four strips.

To prepare the book, start with the second piece of paper in the notebook. Glue one of the pictures to that paper and every other sheet thereafter (pp. 2, 4, 6, etc.). Go back and cut the plain paper (pp. 1, 3, 5, etc.) into three or four equal strips.

Guide the child to turn over one strip of a cut page at a time, which exposes part of the picture. He tries to guess what the picture is about. Can he recognize it with one strip exposed, or does it take two strips or the whole picture before he recognizes it?

—Submitted by Anne H. Smith
Louisville, Kentucky

Choose and Guess

Materials: puzzle, paper sack, and felt-tip marker

Print *Choose and Guess* on the outside of the paper sack. Put the pieces of a puzzle inside the sack. Let preschoolers take turns drawing pieces of the puzzle from the sack, one at a time. After each piece is drawn, allow the child who chose the piece to guess the picture the puzzle will make.

Continue to choose pieces until the puzzle is guessed or until it is assembled. If a child guesses correctly before the puzzle is assembled, let the preschoolers continue to choose and assemble the puzzle.

—Submitted by Rob Sanders
Kansas City, Missouri

What Goes Together?

Materials: an assortment of containers from the kitchen with their lids (cottage cheese, yogurt, sour cream, freezer boxes, margarine tub, etc.); two boxes; dots made from construction paper; and glue

Place matching construction paper dots on each container and lid. For example, a lid has a red dot and its container also has a red dot. Assist the preschoolers who have problems finding the container and lid which go together.

This activity is good for twos and threes, as well as fours and fives.

—Submitted by Carol Miller Kay
Calhoun City, Mississippi

Concentration/Two-of-a-Kind

Materials: fruit or animal sticker-seals and flat metal lids from orange juice cans or plastic snap lids from cans of peanuts, snacks, or powdered drinks

There must be two stickers of each fruit or animal, approximately eight pairs for a game, according to the age of the preschoolers. If the lids have printing on them, cover each lid with a circle of colored self-adhesive plastic to make the backside more attractive. Cut circles of construction paper or self-adhesive plastic to fit into the plastic lids. Paste a seal on each circle and glue to the inside of the lid.

To play the game, the lids are placed face-down on a table or the floor. One child turns up two lids, right-side-up, for each child to see the pictures clearly. If the two lids match, they are removed from the game. If they do not match, the lids are turned facedown in the same spot and left for the next player. Each child tries to remember the location of the pictures so if he later turns up a picture that matches a previously exposed picture, he will know where to find two of a kind. Play continues until all the pairs have been removed from the board.

For variety, games may be made from seal-pictures of flowers, insects, cars, people, houses, etc.

—Submitted by Christine Hackler
Loveland, Ohio

Smile or Frown Decision Game

Materials: two brown paper bags or sacks; three-by-five-inch cards or strips of paper; pencil or pen; and felt-tip markers

On one of the bags, draw a smiling face. On the other one, draw a frowning face. On the cards or paper, print things preschoolers can do at home. Each statement is on a separate card. Examples: *Help mother dust. Take out trash. Pick up my toys. Be kind to a friend. Say thank you. Disobey mother. Leave clothes on the floor. Do not tell the truth. Push a friend.*

Ask preschoolers to make a semicircle, and sit on the floor. Place the bags next to each other with the faces toward the preschoolers. Choose a child to come, choose a card, and then let the adult read the card. Instruct the preschooler to place the card in the appropriate bag, whether that act would lead to a smiling or a frowning face.

—Submitted by Pat Glascock
Little Rock, Arkansas

Pairs of Things

Materials: several pairs of gloves and mittens (real items or pictures of items) and a shopping bag

Place the gloves in various locations around the room. Two preschoolers look for the gloves and place them in the shopping bag as a matching pair is found.

Two other preschoolers may take turns pulling one glove at a time from the shopping bag. As pairs are matched, they are placed together on the floor or table.

Alternate

Put gloves in a paper bag (one for each child present). Prior to group time, each child pulls a glove from the bag, and finds the friend who has its match. Each pair of friends sits together at group time.

—Submitted by Sue M. Perry
Gulfport, Mississippi

Music

"I like to sing."

Teaching Songs Through Pictures

Materials: preschool song books, poster board, glue, and a variety of pictures

Place pictures showing key words of a song on poster board. For example, "Tell Me That God Loves Me," page 45, *More Songs for 4's and 5's*,[1] can have illustrations of birds, flowers, and a bee; sun, wind, and rain; and moon and stars. Preschoolers learn the repetitious words that follow each set of pictures: *Tell me that God loves me.*

[1]Available through Baptist Book Stores.

—Submitted by Nina Edwards
Mustang, Oklahoma

Song: Thank You, Jesus, for Our Food

Sing to the tune of "London Bridge":
>Thank You, Jesus, for our food,
>For our food, for our food.
>Thank You, Jesus, for our food,
>Thank You, Jesus.

Adapt words to make additional verses, such as for friends, family, toys, pets, and church.

—Submitted by Sue Brown
Louisville, Kentucky

Song: This Is the Way

Materials: piano, Autoharp, or song may be unaccompanied

Sing the words and add appropriate motions, to the tune of "Mulberry Bush."
>This is the way we build a church,
>Build a church, build a church.
>This is the way we build a church
>In (name of country or state) today.
>This is the way we plant the seeds . . .
>This is the way we teach the Bible . . .

For variation, the preschoolers may walk in a circle and sing. Following the singing, they stop and imitate the action describe in the verse.

—Submitted by Jane Taylor Howell
Owensboro, Kentucky

Making a Drum

Materials: one oatmeal or salt box per child; colorful self-adhesive plastic; and one-half inch colored plastic tape

Tape the lid on the oatmeal box. Cover the box with self-adhesive plastic. Use the tape to decorate with African or Indian designs. Use for music activities with one preschooler or with a group.

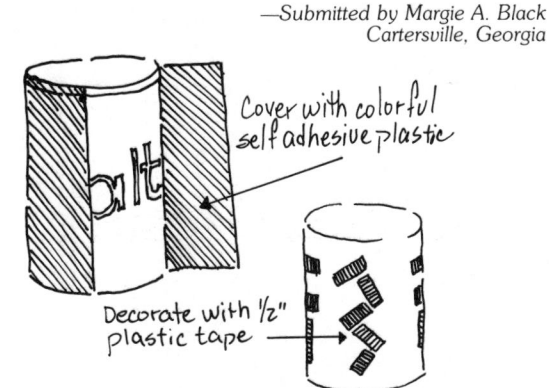

—Submitted by Margie A. Black
Cartersville, Georgia

Rhythms

Materials: record player and recording of music with a steady beat

Play the recording. Suggest that the preschoolers clap in rhythm. Vary keeping the beat by: tapping toes, snapping fingers, tapping thighs, etc.

Explain that everyone's name has a rhythm. Say a name. Repeat it while clapping the syllables. Continue this activity until every child's name has been clapped. Say: Thank You, God, for ears which let us hear rhythm.

—Submitted by Sharon B. Garnett
Chesapeake, Virginia

Paper-Plate Shakers

Materials: for each shaker use one large craft stick, two dessert-size paper plates, crepe paper, small gravel or rocks, crayons, stapler with staples, and glue

Staple the craft stick to the inside of a paper plate, one staple near the center of the plate, and one staple near the edge of the plate. The preschooler colors a design on the back of the other plate. Then staple the colored plate to the handled plate all the way around, except for an opening left to fill with pebbles or gravel. After filling, close the opening with staples.

Give each child four crepe-paper strips about 7 inches long to glue or staple to the edges of the shakers.

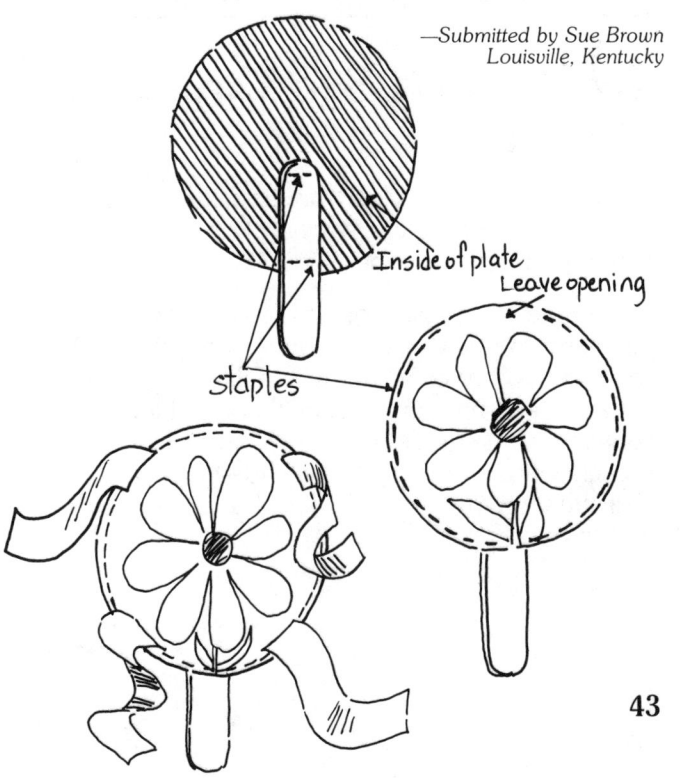

—Submitted by Sue Brown
Louisville, Kentucky

Making Rhythm Sticks

Materials: four double sheets of newspaper for each child; masking tape; picture of musical instruments; and a recording of marching music such as *Everyday Rhythms for Children*[1]

Demonstrate how to make the rhythm sticks. Fold two sheets of newspaper in half. Begin rolling from the bottom corner of the folded side, and roll tightly. When completely rolled, tape edges securely with several pieces of masking tape. Listen to the music and encourage preschoolers to march around as they play their rhythm sticks.

Look at the picture of musical instruments and talk about ways to make music with each instrument.

[1]Available through Baptist Book Stores.

—Submitted by Cris Williamson
Macon, Georgia

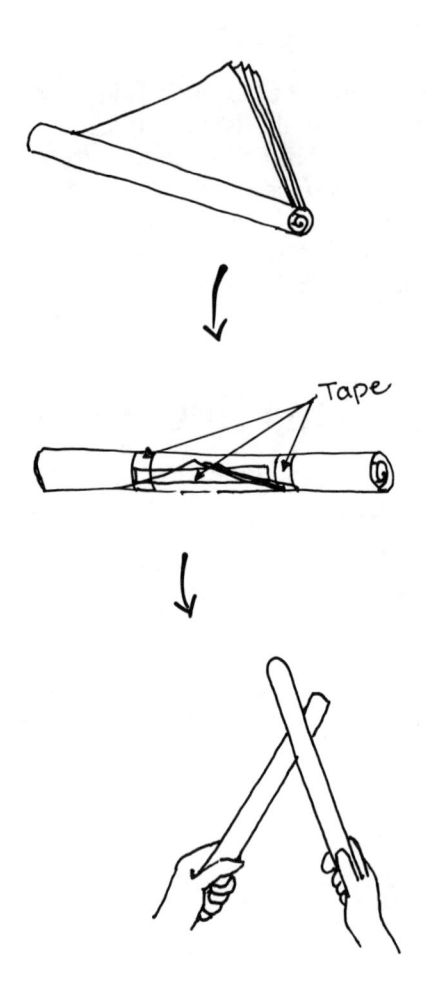

Two Sounds See-Through Shaker

Materials: two large clear, plastic pill containers with lids or two acrylic cubes; plastic milk lids; pebbles; and plastic tape.

Encourage one preschooler to place some of the pebbles into one of the containers. Another child can fill the other container with milk lids. Let the preschoolers snap on the container lids. Hold the containers together lid to lid. Overlap the tape in a circle around the containers to secure them. Call attention to the different sound made by each end of the shaker.

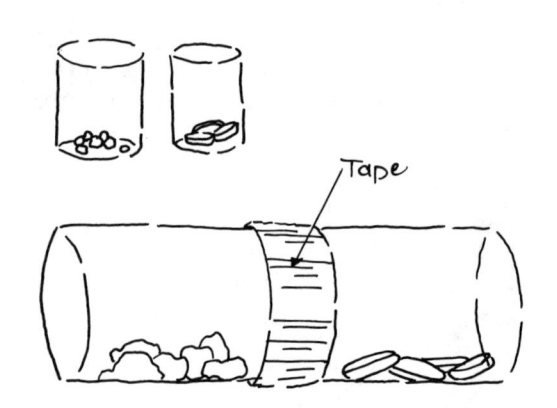

—Submitted by Lillian Hill
Waco, Texas

Shakers

Materials: empty toilet-tissue rolls, masking tape, gravel or sand, and crayons

Make shakers by taping closed one end of each tissue roll. Let each preschooler place a small amount of sand or gravel in each roll. Then, close the other end with tape. Crayons may be used to decorate the shaker. Preschoolers enjoy these instruments because they fit their hands.

Alternate

A shaker may be made from two matching aerosol can lids and colorful plastic tape. Place gravel in one lid, glue the other lid on top, and seal with the tape.

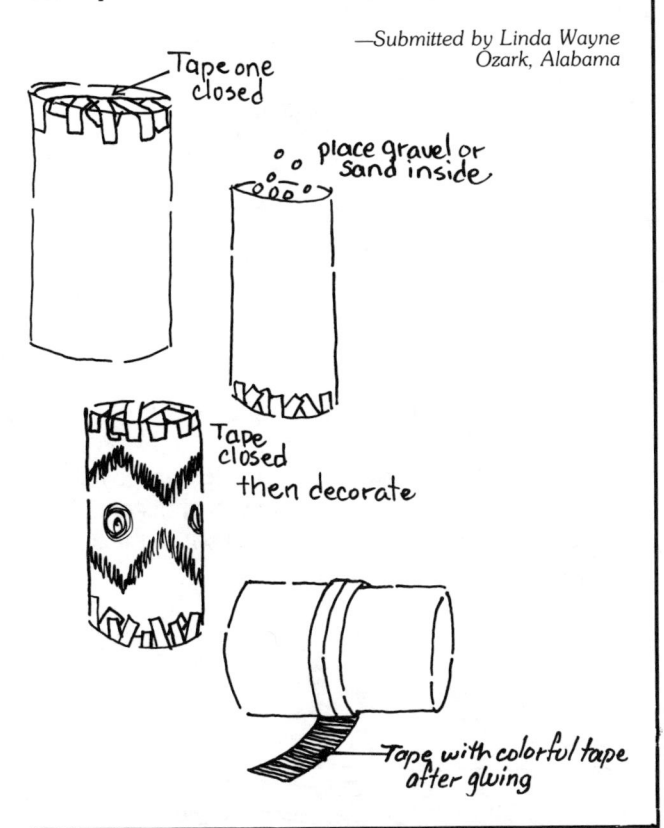

—Submitted by Linda Wayne
Ozark, Alabama

Creative Streamers

Materials: instrumental recording, record player, and 3 18-inch long crepe-paper streamers per child

Give each child three streamers. Play the recording. Encourage the preschoolers to walk, run, skip, or jump while holding the streamers.

—Submitted by Susan Hardison
Washington, Vermont

Downbeat

Materials: recording of music in ¾ time; one 9-by-12-inch piece of bright colored construction paper; clear self-adhesive plastic; scissors; and record player

Apply the clear self-adhesive plastic to the sheet of construction paper. Fold the prepared paper in half. Cut a free-hand circle about 6 inches in diameter. Cut a spiraling line to the center, making the strip about ½ half inch wide. Make a circle for each child and teacher.

On the first day, lay the circles on the floor to conceal the spiral cut. Select a child with rhythmical abilities to help introduce the activity. Place your finger on the inside tab and say: Pick up the circle here.

Pick up your circle at the same time and allow preschoolers to see it fall into the spiral. Ask: How can we move these circles?

Allow the child to demonstrate and imitate in up-and-down motions. Try the same movement with the other hand and say *down* when the hand is in the lowest position. Give out the other circles so that others can participate.

The second time this is used, review the action briefly and then play a recording. Ask the preschoolers to say *down* on the strong beat of one. They may count with each measure: down, 2 3, down, 2 3.

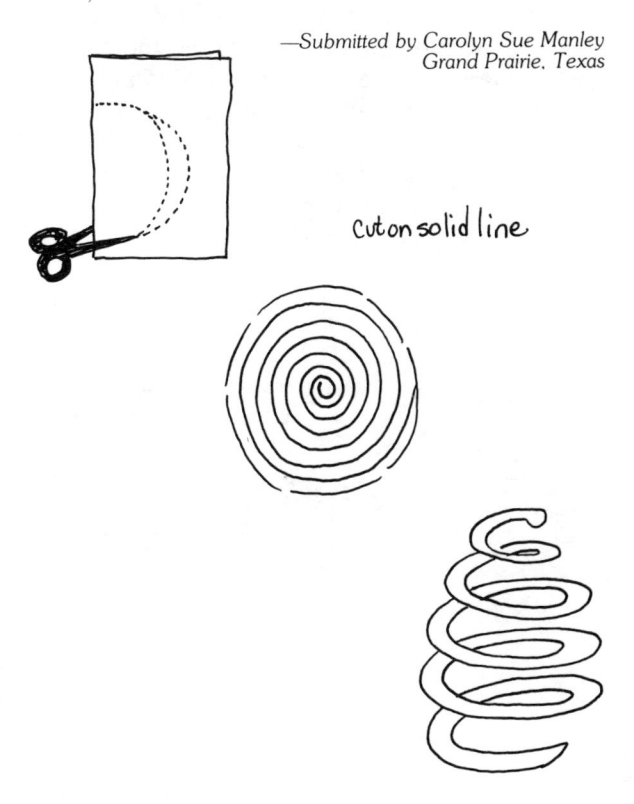

—Submitted by Carolyn Sue Manley
Grand Prairie, Texas

45

Music

Turtle Walk

Materials: 12 pieces of construction paper or cardboard 2 inches square; crayons or felt-tip markers; and a paper bag

Draw a turtle walking on each of 6 squares of construction paper. On the other 6 squares draw a turtle in his shell (resting). Place all 12 squares in a paper bag.

Lead a preschooler to draw 4 squares and place them in any order he chooses. Explain that when you point to a walking card he is to say *walk*. When you point to a resting card, he is to say *rest*. Establish a four-beat rhythm, and ask the child to say in rhythm the appropriate word (*walk* or *rest*) as you point to the pictures, such as: *walk, walk, walk, rest*. Many different rhythmic patterns can be established by drawing different cards and rearranging cards.

—Submitted by Sandi Keown
Franklin, Tennessee

Ham-Can Banjo

Materials: one ham can with lid removed, three rubber bands of different thicknesses, heavy tape, and an empty paper-towel roll

Cover the sharp edges of the can with masking tape. Attach the paper towel roll to the ham can with tape at the narrow end of the can. Attach the rubber bands with the smallest first and the heaviest one last. Tape each band at each end, pulling it tightly across the opening of the can. Preschoolers will enjoy playing the banjo and experimenting with musical sounds.

Alternate

A simple instrument may be made from a small shoe box with the lid removed. Cover the outside of the shoe box with construction paper or a colored self-adhesive plastic. Wrap eight large rubber bands around the box, roughly equidistant. Provide some thin rubber bands and some thick ones to produce different tones.

—Submitted by Carol Miller Kay
Calhoun City, Mississippi

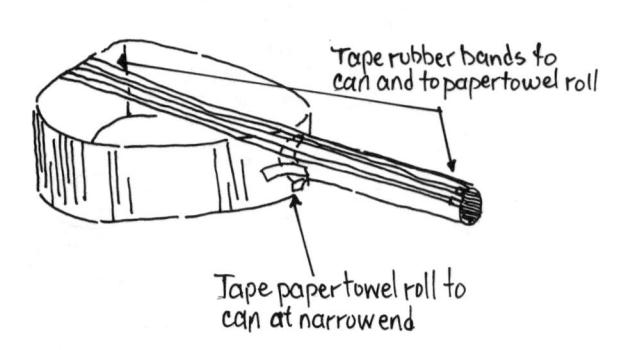

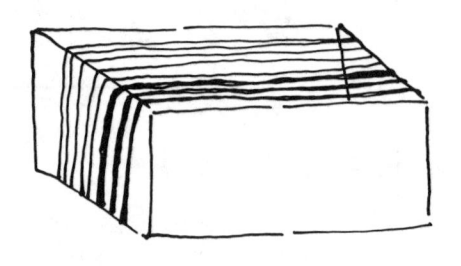

Movement Patterns

Materials: drum and tambourine

Ask the preschoolers to show how an elephant walks. Duplicate movement with drum beats. Ask the preschoolers to show how soldiers march. Duplicate this movement/rhythm with the drum. When they show how ponies gallop, pick up the rhythm with the drum. Ask them to show how leaves softly fall. Gently shake the tambourine as they whirl and fall.

Preschoolers can take turns duplicating the rhythm with the instruments. After this experience, initiate the rhythm with an instrument, and let the preschoolers demonstrate it with body movement.

—Submitted by Nina Joseph
Mobile, Alabama

Who's Got the Chicken? Who's Got the Egg?

Materials: small plastic egg and small toy chicken

Sit with preschoolers in a circle. Hand one child the chicken and another the egg. Everyone sings or chants: Who's got the chicken, who's got the egg?

As the preschoolers sing, they pass the egg and the chicken. Whoever ends up with the chicken at the end of the song shows it and sings: I've got the chicken.

Whoever has the egg shows it and sings: I've got the egg.

Repeat this as many times as desired.

—Submitted by Brenda Sue Hall
Brentwood, Maryland

Feel the Beat

Materials: any song (recording or sung a capella) may be used with this activity

As preschoolers sing or listen to a song, say: Feel the beat in your legs.

Guide the preschoolers to tap their knees with their hands to the rhythm of the music. Continue the activity by "Feeling" the beat elsewhere . . . on your head, on your stomach, on your shoulders, etc.

—Submitted by Rob Sanders
Kansas City, Missouri

Dial-a-Song

Materials: two sheets of poster board, small pictures that suggest familiar songs, and a brad

Cut pictures to a four-by-six-inch size. Cut one poster board into a large circle. Glue the pictures around the edge of the circle. Cut the other poster board to the same size circle, and cut a four-by-six-inch section at one edge. Fasten the two circles together at the center with a brad so that the open section will expose a picture as the top circle is turned.

Lead the preschoolers to take turns turning the top wheel to expose a picture, then tell what song it suggests. Lead preschoolers to sing the song.

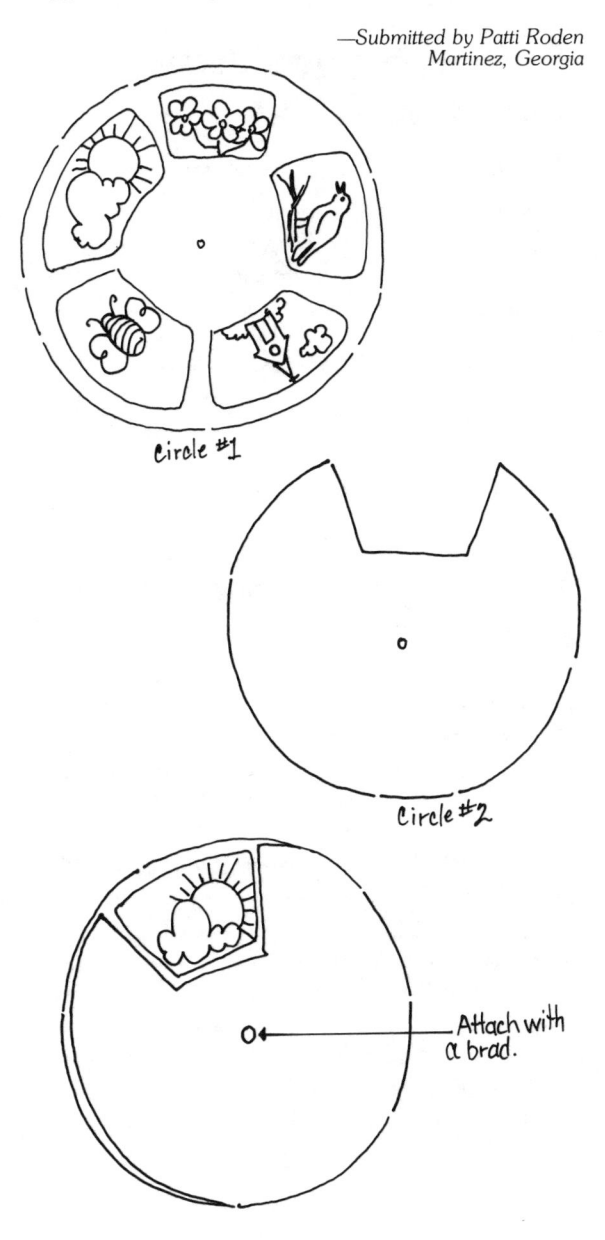

—Submitted by Patti Roden
Martinez, Georgia

Driving Along the Highway

Materials: child-size chair and the song "Driving Along the Highway," page 79, *Songs for the Young Child*[1]

Choose one child to sit in a chair. All of the boys and girls sing the song. At the end of the song, the child sitting in the chair substitutes a child's name for the word *I*. The child named gets to sit in the chair. Continue the game.

[1]Available through Baptist Book Stores.

—Submitted by Cornelia Branton Turrittin
Hampton, Virginia

Action Songs Using Familiar Tunes

Tune: "Are You Sleeping?"

Teacher: Who has red on? Who has red on?
  Who is wearing red? Who is wearing red?
Preschoolers: We are wearing red. We are wearing red. We wear red; we wear red.

The teacher tells the boys and girls that when they have on the color mentioned in the song, they are to stand and sing the response. Adapt the words of the song to the colors observed in the clothing of the group.

Tune: "A Hunting We Will Go" (Circle Game)

Around we will go, around we will go,
Around in a circle now, around we will go.
(Move around in a circle while holding hands.)
To the center we will go, to the center we will go,
Now clap and clap and clap your hands, Now touch a toe
(Move to the center of the circle, clap hands, and touch toe.)
Around we will go, around we will go,
Around in a circle now, around we will go.
(Move around in a circle while holding hands.)
Reach very high, and stoop very low.
Stand up straight, and clap your hands, turn around just so.
(Stop, stretch high, stoop, clap hands, and turn around.)

Tune: "Do You Know the Muffin Man?"

Let's all play the standing game,
The standing game, the standing game.
Let's all play the standing game,
Everybody stand.

Adapt this song to the action you would like for the boys and girls to follow, such as walking, marching, clapping, hopping, tiptoe, etc.

Tune: "Mary Had a Little Lamb"

Will you come and walk with me, walk with me, walk with me?
Will you come and walk with me, all around the room?

Add other verses and actions; such as jog, fly, swim, skate, etc.

48

Games

"I want to play."

It's Me!

Materials: hand mirror

Sit with preschoolers in a circle. Tell them that each will have a turn to look at himself in the hand mirror and say something nice about what she sees. The leader may set the example by looking in the mirror and saying: My name is Mrs. Jones, and I have blue eyes.

Hand the mirror to a child in the circle and ask the child to say something nice about himself. Continue until each child has a turn. This game is good to help develop a positive self-image.

—Submitted by Brenda Price
Louisville, Kentucky

The Color Game

Materials: different colors of construction paper or poster board

Cut about 10 or 12 circles (10-14 inches in diameter) from the construction paper or poster board. Place the circles on the floor with masking tape underneath to keep them in place. The teacher calls the name of a fruit, vegetable, or other object that is the color of one of the circles on the floor. Preschoolers then rush to stand on the circle that is the color of the object named. There may be more than one answer, as apples are red, green, and sometimes yellow.

—Submitted by Susan Hardison
Washington, Vermont

Hot or Cold Climates

Materials: pictures of tools and clothes used in hot or cold weather

The child sorts the clothes and tools, deciding what is used in a hot or a cold climate.

—Submitted by Jane Taylor Howell
Owensboro, Kentucky

Name the Animal

Materials: broad felt-tip marker; typing paper; coloring book with animals in it, and 9-by-12-inch brown envelope

Trace the outline of several animals from the coloring book onto typing paper with the felt-tip marker. Place these in the envelope so the feet are closest to the opening.

Tell the preschoolers that in the envelope you have pictures of animals and that you will show them the feet to see if they can guess each animal. Slowly pull one picture at a time out of the envelope until the animal's feet are showing. If the animal is not guessed, continue to pull the picture out of the envelope. Conversation may include God's plan for animals or how each one is different.

—Submitted by Zadabeth Uland
Plano, Texas

Mystery Sock Box

Materials: one tall oatmeal box and one discarded tube sock (colorful trim or stripes desirable)

Make a durable and unique mystery (or guess) box for preschoolers to use. Carefully pull an old tube sock up and around the empty cardboard oatmeal box. The sock will fit snugly on the box.

The mystery box may be filled with safe, familiar objects. Ask a child to put his hand through the sock, down into the box, feel an object, and try to guess what it is. (The top of the tube sock will fit snugly around the child's arm and prevent him from seeing the object.)

Tube Pumping

Materials: large inner tube (truck tire, if possible) and hand air pump

The preschoolers take turns pumping up the tube. This is an activity that teaches working together and cooperation. This can be an inside or outside activity. The pumped-up tube may be used for sitting and jumping.

—Submitted by Martha Harless
Enid, Oklahoma

Who Will Ride the Train?

Materials: child-size chairs and scrap paper to use for tickets

The teacher begins placing chairs in a line, one behind the other, singing to any tune: Who will ride the train, who will ride the train?

As preschoolers begin to sit down, sing their names: Jim will ride the train, Kara will ride the train, etc., until each child has been named.

The teacher is the engineer and conductor in the beginning, but as preschoolers become familiar with the game, they can take turns. When everyone who wants to play is seated in a chair, the conductor calls *All Aboard*, then takes the front chair to drive the train. The teacher rings the bell and toots the whistle, then starts moving arms like the wheels on a train, slowly at first, then faster and faster. Then slow down and end with blowing out air, like the air brakes on the train and letting arms hang loosely. Preschoolers follow these motions. Then the conductor goes down the line handing out tickets. Say: This is your ticket; don't lose your ticket.

Repeat the train motions. Then take up the tickets, tearing each in half—keeping one half, and giving the other back to the passenger. Comment about who the person is and where that person is going, such as: This is Tara. She's going to Kansas to visit Grandma.

As preschoolers leave the train, each gives the conductor the other half of the ticket.

—Submitted by Neva Starnes
Delta Junction, Alaska

Choosing a Song or Prayer Request

Materials: large cube, papered or painted in bright colors (different color on each side)

Paste or tape a song or prayer request on each side of the cube. Use all sides.

A child rolls the cube gently. The song or request that comes out on top is the one the group sings or prays for that time.

—Submitted by Jane Taylor Howell
Owensboro, Kentucky

Spin the Can

Materials: tall potato-chip can with lid, construction paper, Bible thoughts, activity ideas, and scissors

Cut the construction paper into strips to fit inside the can. Print in manuscript letters a Bible thought or activity on each strip. Activities could include: Give a friend a hug; name something God made; stand up and clap your hands three times; walk to the door and back.

Place the strips in the can, and fasten the lid.

Preschoolers sit in a circle. Spin the can. The person the can top points to takes out a strip and says the Bible thought, which the teacher reads and whispers into the preschooler's ear. If the strip has an acitivity on it, the teacher reads the instructions aloud and the child responds by doing the action.

—Submitted by Cheryl G. Davis
Lilburn, Georgia

Tell a Story

Materials: 6 groups of 3 pictures each, each group telling a story with a beginning, middle, and end (cut pictures from magazines, outdated church literature, etc.); 18 3-by-5 cards; glue; clear self-adhesive plastic; scissors; and 6 business envelopes

Cut 6 sets of 3 sequential pictures from magazines. Each set of pictures should tell a story. Glue the pictures on 3-by-5 cards. Cover the front of the cards with clear, self-adhesive plastic for durability. Place each set of pictures in an envelope.

A child takes an envelope, examines the pictures, and places the cards in order (sequence) from left to right to tell a story. The preschoolers take turns to tell the story represented on the cards.

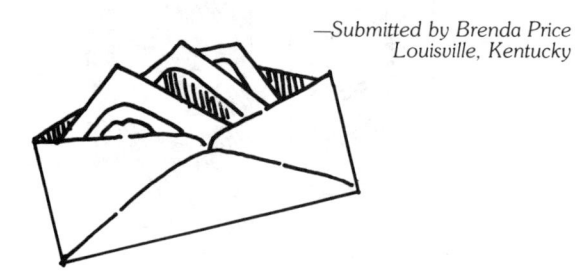

—Submitted by Brenda Price
Louisville, Kentucky

Ways Missionaries Travel

Materials: pictures of ways missionaries travel, such as car, pickup truck, van, jeep, recreational vehicle, snowmobile, train, bus, ship, boat, canoe, motorcycle, bicycle, airplane, horse, burro; poster board; scissors; and glue

Mount the pictures on poster-board pieces cut to the same size.

Explain to the boys and girls that you have pictures of ways missionaries travel and that you will tell them about the picture to see if they can guess one way missionaries travel. Give details of each vehicle without calling the name of the transportation. Encourage the preschoolers to guess the vehicle.

The game may also be played by giving each child a picture. Each child is to demonstrate to the others one way missionaries travel, without showing the picture to anyone.

Concluding conversation may emphasize that some of our money given to the church helps missionaries travel to places they need to go.

—Submitted by Zadabeth Uland
Plano, Texas

Riddle Game

Materials: pictures of snow, clouds, rainbow, evidence of wind, sun, and moon; poster board; scissors; and glue

Glue pictures on 10-by-12-inch pieces of poster board. As the teacher reads a riddle, the preschoolers find the picture that answers it, or preschoolers can just guess the answer after you read the riddle.

While we were asleep
One cold winter night,
God sent a surprise
All fluffy and white. (*snow*)

We are white and puffy;
We are big and fluffy;
We bring shade and rain;
We never look the same. (*clouds*)

I am many pretty colors
Way up in the sky,
And only God can make me
After rain falls from the sky. (*rainbow*)

You can never see me
As I travel through the town.
I take leaves off the trees
And blow them all over the ground. (*wind*)

God made me to light the night.
To watch me at night
Is such a delight. (*moon and stars*)

I am round and yellow,
I am warm and bright.
I shine in the daytime
And hide at night. (*sun*)

—Submitted by Nina Edwards
Mustang, Oklahoma

Fishing

Materials: poster board, clear self-adhesive plastic, large paper clips, magnet, heavy string, 18-inch bamboo pole, and plastic dishpan

Cut poster board into fish shapes. Cover with self-adhesive plastic. Attach large paper clips to the shapes. Tie string to the top of the bamboo pole. Attach a magnet to the end of the string. Place fish in the dishpan. Preschoolers catch fish as the magnet attracts the paper clips. (Fish may have a Bible thought attached or a question about the unit of study.)

—Submitted by Margie A. Black
Cartersville, Georgia

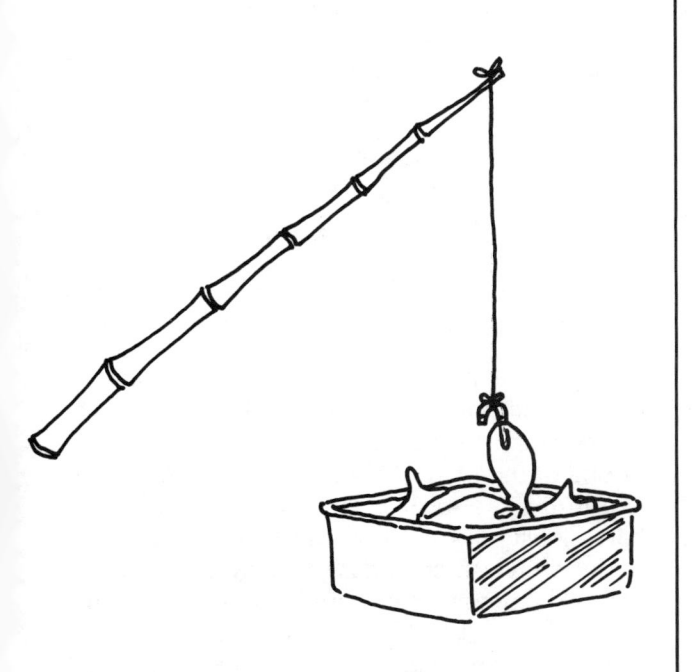

Box-Ball-Action

Materials: three cardboard boxes or containers of various sizes; one beanbag, spongeball, or soft plastic ball; and three-by-five-inch cards or slips of paper

On each of the cards, print questions from the story, if this game is used as a review. Write specific actions the preschooler can do. Each action should be written on a separate slip. Examples: *touch your toes; wave your hands; nod your head; hop on both feet; smile; wiggle your fingers; frown; turn around; hop on one foot.* The teacher holds the slips.

To play the game: A child tries to throw the ball into one of the boxes or containers. If she gets it in the box or container, she gets to choose a slip and do one of the actions or answer the question. The boxes or containers are arranged to give the preschooler a good chance to succeed.

—Submitted by Pat Glascock
Little Rock, Arkansas

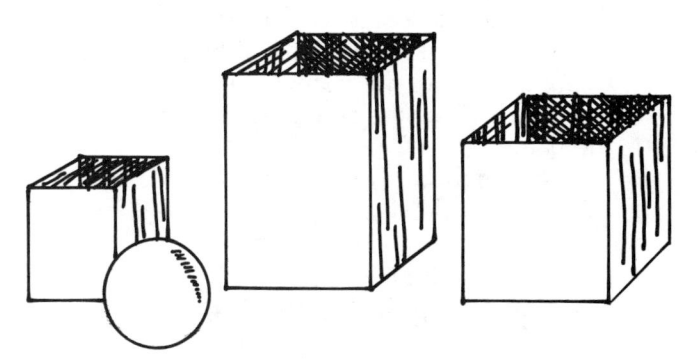

Hello!

Choose a child to be "It." Place that one with his back to the group. Ask "It" to close his eyes. Choose another child, without calling the name aloud, to tap "It" on the shoulder, then say *hello*, and return to his chair. "It" turns around and tries to guess who tapped him on the shoulder. (Foreign words may be substituted for *hello*. For example: *jambo* [JAHM-boh] which is Swahili spoken in several African countries; *bonjour* [bohn-JOOR], French; and *hola* [OH-lah], Spanish.)

—Submitted by Pat Glascock
Little Rock, Arkansas

Pretend and Stretch

Lead the preschoolers to pretend to be different things that will allow them to stretch and move. Older preschoolers may be able to lead as they volunteer to do so. Examples: Teacher says, "Let's pretend to be a tall tree blowing in the wind." They stand on tiptoe, hold arms over their heads, and move torsos from side to side.

"Let's pretend to be a short bush." They move to a squatting position.

"Let's pretend to be a frog." They leap around.

"Let's pretend to be a rabbit." They hop.

—Submitted by Pat Glascock
Little Rock, Arkansas

Egg Carton—Numeral Recognition

Materials: egg carton, marble, felt-tip marker

Write a different numeral inside each holder of a plastic-foam egg carton. Place a marble inside the carton and close the lid. Invite an older preschooler to shake the carton. When the carton is opened, identify the numeral where the marble is located. Close the carton, shake, and continue the game.

For variation, use colors for middle preschoolers to identify.

—Submitted by Dixie Ruth Crase
Memphis, Tennessee

Concentration

Materials: magazines, wallpaper books, catalogs, or seals; poster board; glue or paste; clear self-adhesive plastic; and scissors

Cut poster board into two- or three-inch squares. Find two matching pictures or patterns and glue each to a square. Cover each square with clear self-adhesive plastic for durability. Make several sets, according to the ages of the preschoolers. Fours and fives may handle as many as six or seven pairs.

To play the game, place the squares face down in rows. The preschooler selects two. If they match, he may keep the set; if not, he turns them back face down. Another player has a turn.

The squares may be related to a variety of subjects. This game can be used in nature, home-living, puzzles, or for a relaxation activity, depending on the pictures or designs on the squares.

—Submitted by Elsie M. McCall
Mill Valley, California

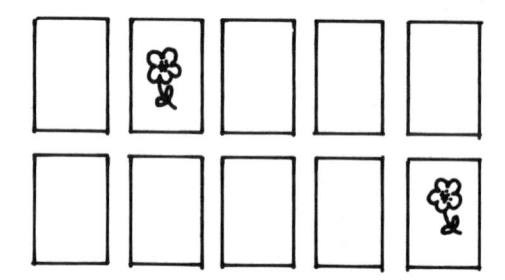

Hiding Snowballs

Materials: small, white Styrofoam ball; rubber ball; white, round beanbag; or other similar object

Choose three preschoolers to stand in a line, side-by-side with their hands behind their backs. The teacher then tries to put the ball into the hands of one of the preschoolers without the others sitting in the group observing which child has the ball. Finally, ask the boys and girls in the group to decide which child has the snowball. After the ball is discovered, three more preschoolers may be chosen until all have had a turn.

This game may be adapted to any unit by hiding an object common to that area. (The Styrofoam ball represents winter and snow.)

—Submitted by Eloise Stinchcomb
Randallstown, Maryland

Relaxing

Materials: projector, filmstrip or slides of nature subjects, instrumental recording, and record player

Have preschoolers recline on a mat or carpet. Darken the room. Show a filmstrip on the ceiling with soft music to accompany it. (Slides and projector may be used.)

—Submitted by Jennifer Cox
Birmingham, Alabama

Music Mirroring

Materials: a quiet, listening recording

Instruct the preschoolers to sit on the floor with enough space between them to move their arms. As the music softly plays, they move their arms in slow, large movements. Preschoolers may mirror the movements of the leader. Boys and girls may take turns being the leader.

—Submitted by Rob Sanders
Kansas City, Missouri

The Color of My Clothes

This is a group game to help preschoolers recognize and name colors. Call out a color and an item of clothing, such as white shoes, blue socks, or red shirt. Preschoolers wearing these items stand up or follow directions, such as walk around the circle, stoop, and touch your toes.

—Submitted by Carol Kay
Calhoun City, Mississippi

Kick the Jug

Materials: clean plastic gallon milk jugs with tops on them

Take preschoolers outside. Place a number of the jugs around the play area for them to kick. After running and kicking for a while, the preschoolers will be relaxed and ready for inside again.

—Submitted by Katherine Hooks
Bowling Green, Kentucky

Look at Me

Hands in your lap now one, two, three.
Feet on the floor. It's easy, don't you see?
Smile on your face bright as can be.
Now, turn around and look at me.

—Submitted by Sue Brown
Louisville, Kentucky

Adam and Eve (Finger Play)

God made Adam. (*Raise one finger on one hand.*)
God made Eve. (*Raise one finger on the other hand.*)
All the people (*Raise all fingers.*)
Came from these.

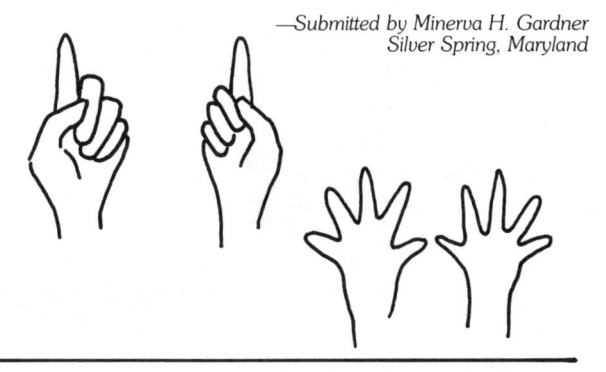

—Submitted by Minerva H. Gardner
Silver Spring, Maryland

Relaxation

Recite the rhyme and do the actions. Encourage preschoolers to follow along.

> Hands on your hips.
> Hands on your knees.
> Put them behind you,
> If you please.
>
> Touch your shoulder;
> Now your toes.
> Touch your eyes;
> And then your nose.
>
> Hold your hands high
> Up in the air;
> Down at your sides;
> Now touch your hair.
>
> Hold your hands
> High up as before,
> Now you may clap,
> One, two, three, four!

—Submitted by Lucy Bateman
Dallas, Texas

Picture-Cube Toss

Materials: cardboard box, about four-inches square; glue; magazine pictures showing people being kind and helpful; construction paper; scissors; and clear self-adhesive plastic

Cover the box with construction paper. Cut out the pictures, and glue one on each of the six sides. Cover the box with clear self-adhesive plastic for durability.

To play the game, a teacher gives a clue about one of the pictures. Then she tosses the picture cube to a child and asks the child to find the picture described.

Depending on the maturity of the preschoolers, boys and girls may take turns describing a picture for a friend to find.

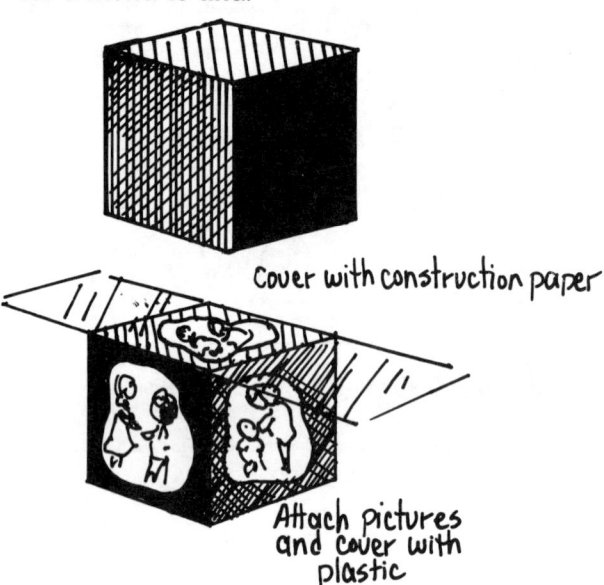

Alternate Use of Picture Cube

Play a Bible thought game. Place bookmarks at these thoughts: A friend loves at all times (see Prov. 17:17); Be kind to one another (see Eph. 4:32); Help one another (see Gal. 5:13); Love one another (see 1 John 4:7); We are helpers (see 2 Cor. 1:24); and We work together (see 1 Cor. 3:9).

Ask a child to choose a bookmark. Read the thought. Ask him to find a picture on the cube that reminds him of the Bible thought.

Using the picture cube can stimulate conversation with the child about ways missionaries help others and that God wants us to love and help other people.

—Submitted by Linda Hurley
Centerville, Ohio

Guess the Instrument

Materials: a cardboard box, approximately 12-by-24 inches in size; and several rhythm instruments, such as a triangle, a tambourine, a set of sticks, and a small drum

Turn the box on one side. Place the instruments inside the box without the preschoolers seeing them. Instruct the boys and girls to listen and then guess the sound they hear. Carefully place the box on your lap with the bottom of the box toward the preschoolers. Play each instrument inside the box as the boys and girls guess what makes the sound they hear. After each instrument is guessed correctly, show and demonstrate it.

—Submitted by Zadabeth Uland
Plano, Texas

Wiggle Game

Materials: one sheet of construction paper or typing paper for each child or a floor covered with tile squares

Direct preschoolers to place both their feet in one square on the floor, or give each child a sheet of paper on which he places both feet. Tell them they can wiggle any part of their bodies as long as they keep their feet on the square or their paper. Encourage wiggling by asking: Can you wiggle your toes? What about your ankles? Your knees? Your hips?

Move up the body. Conclude by commenting about God's plan for our bodies to move, if this conversation seems appropriate.

—Submitted by Zadabeth Uland
Plano, Texas

Colors

Materials: different colors of beanbags

Use only four colors with middle preschoolers. More colors may be used with older preschoolers.

Toss a beanbag to a child, and ask him to name something God made that color (blue—sky) or something they saw on their way to church that was the color of the beanbag.

Another variation is to mark Bible thoughts with the same colors as the beanbags. The child can choose the verse marked with his color.

—Submitted by Bonnie Woodard
Louisville, Kentucky

Recipes

"I can cook."

Chinese Ting-a-Lings

Materials: 2 6-ounce packages of butterscotch morsels; 1 5-ounce can of chow mein noodles; tablespoon; hot plate and double boiler; several plastic spoons; and waxed paper

Suggest that the preschoolers place the butterscotch morsels in the boiler. The adult will melt the morsels in the top of the double boiler, stirring constantly. When melted, remove from the heat. Guide the preschoolers to add the noodles and stir. Let them drop the mixture by teaspoonful onto waxed paper to cool and set. Enjoy!

—Submitted by Hilda Dalzell
Lexington, Kentucky
and
Nina Edwards
Mustang, Oklahoma

Doughnuts

Materials: any type of canned biscuit, confectioners sugar, cinnamon sugar, oil, electric skillet, spatula, and napkins

All preschoolers participating wash their hands. Divide the canned biscuit dough in half, giving each preschooler one half. Show them how to roll the dough into a ball. Allow them to watch their doughnuts being fried in the skillet. When golden brown, remove doughnuts and allow to cool slightly. Lead the preschoolers to roll the doughnuts in either confectioners sugar or cinnamon and sugar. Place the doughnuts on napkins to serve for a snack.

—Submitted by Gail Skipper Guyton
New Orleans, Lousiana

Biscuit Pizza

Materials: canned biscuits, pizza sauce, mozzarella cheese, waxed paper, cookie sheet, and small oven

Preschoolers should wash hands before beginning this activity. Guide the preschoolers to press and flatten the biscuits on a sheet of waxed paper, then put them on a cookie sheet. Help preschoolers add sauce, then sprinkle the cheese on top. Each preschooler may grate his own cheese.

Bake biscuits at 375°F for 10-15 minutes or until edges are lightly browned.

—Submitted by Steve Peek
Knoxville, Tennessee

Gingerbread People

Materials: 1 stick margarine, 1 egg, 1 cup flour, ¾ cup water, 1 cup brown sugar, 2 boxes gingerbread mix, 2 large mixing bowls, 2 cookie sheets, stove, cookie cutters, waxed paper, cooling racks, and spoons

Guide the preschoolers to combine the gingerbread mix and flour in a mixing bowl. Help them measure and mix the margarine, brown sugar, and egg in another bowl.

Help the preschoolers mix the contents of both bowls together, slowly adding ¾ cup water. Lead the preschoolers to take turns stirring until contents are completely blended. Turn the dough out on waxed paper and allow preschoolers to pat it to ¼ to ⅛ inch thick. Suggest that the preschoolers take turns using the cookie cutters to cut out gingerbread people. Place the gingerbread people on a cookie sheet and bake at 350°F for 12-15 minutes.

Use other cookie-cutter shapes, as desired.

—Submitted by Larry Dangerfield
Fort Worth, Texas

Brazilian Baked Bananas

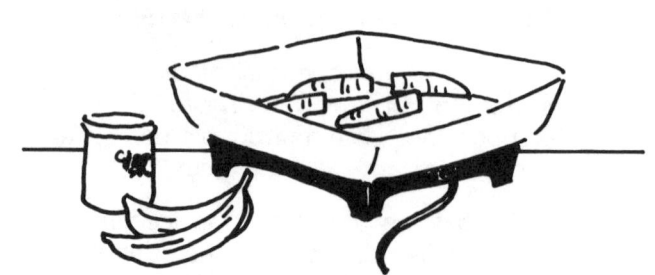

Materials: bananas (one for every two preschoolers); plastic knives; butter or margarine; cinnamon and sugar; toaster oven or electric skillet; spatula; plates; napkins; and baking pan

Guide preschoolers to wash hands. Lead them to peel the bananas and cut them in half crosswise. Then they cut them in half again, lengthwise. Place in a baking pan or in the electric skillet. Place butter on each banana section. Sprinkle each section with cinnamon and sugar. Let preschoolers place the baking pan in the toaster oven or turn on the skillet. Bake at 350°F for 15-20 minutes. Serve on plates.

Animal-Cracker Sandwiches

Materials: animal crackers, peanut butter, plastic knives, and napkins

Place several animal crackers on a napkin. Lead the preschoolers to choose two crackers that are alike and spread peanut butter on one, then fit the other cracker on top to make a sandwich.

—Submitted by Nell Branum
Mount Olive, Alabama

Making Pudding

Materials: any flavor of instant pudding, milk, measuring cup, spoon, rotary beater, small paper cups, refrigerator, and plastic spoons

Guide the preschoolers to measure the milk and add the pudding mix. Lead them to take turns stirring and using the rotary beater. Pour the pudding into paper cups and let each preschooler take his cup to the refrigerator to chill. Provide plastic spoons so that pudding may be eaten later for a snack.

—Submitted by Mrs. Fred Halbrooks
Louisville, Kentucky

Creamy Candy

Materials: 1 box of dry frosting mix, 2 sticks of butter or margarine, 1 teaspoon vanilla, chopped nuts, and a bowl

Set the butter out to soften. Mix softened butter in a bowl with the frosting mix and the vanilla. Let preschoolers use their hands (washed) to knead the mixture until it is well mixed. Roll pieces of the mixture into small balls. Roll the balls in the chopped nuts.

—Submitted by Gayle Lintz
Waco, Texas

Peanut Butter

Materials: 1 cup dry-roasted peanuts, 1 tablespoon salad oil, salt to taste, and food processor

Place steel blade in food processor bowl. Add peanuts, cover, and process until nuts make butter of the texture desired. Gradually add oil to achieve consistency to spread.

—Submitted by Lynda B. Mills
Pasadena, Texas

Easy Candy

Materials: 2 cups confectioners sugar, sifted; ¼ cup cocoa (optional); ¼ cup peanut butter; 2 tablespoons evaporated milk; bowl; spoon; waxed paper; rolling pin; and knife

Guide preschoolers to mix all the ingredients in the bowl. Put the mound of dough between waxed paper and roll out. Set aside to harden. Cut into small squares.

—Submitted by Lucy Bateman
Dallas, Texas

Peanut Butter Balls

Materials: 1 small jar peanut butter, 1 jar marshmallow cream, graham cracker crumbs, large bowl, small bowl, spoon, and waxed paper

Guide preschoolers to mix peanut butter and marshmallow cream in a large bowl. Have them stir and knead until smooth. Let them roll the dough into small balls and roll the balls in graham cracker crumbs. Place the balls on waxed paper.

Variation

Mix ½ cup peanut butter, ¼ cup honey, and 2 cups powdered milk together. Roll the mixture into balls. Place on a plate and serve.

—Submitted by Margie A. Black
Cartersville, Georgia

No-Bake Peanut Butter Cookies

Materials: ½ cup honey or corn syrup; ½ cup peanut butter; 3 cups crisp rice cereal; plastic mixing bowl; wooden spoon, and waxed paper

The preschoolers may take turns mixing the honey or corn syrup with the peanut butter in a bowl. Add the rice cereal. Suggest that the boys and girls take turn stirring with a wooden spoon. Put a small spoonful into a child's clean hands and suggest that she roll it into a ball. Lead her to lay the ball on waxed paper and press down to form a flat, round cookie. Cookie is ready to eat.

—Submitted by Cris Williamson
Macon, Georgia

Cup-Cake Cones

Materials: 1 box cake mix; ingredients to add to mix as called for on the box; 1 tub ready-to-spread frosting; 16-25 ice cream cones; baking sheet; mixing bowl; spoon; candy sprinkles; oven; and plastic knives

Guide preschoolers to measure and stir the ingredients called for in the cake-mix directions. Pour the batter into ice cream cones which have been placed on a baking sheet. Fill cones about ⅔ full. Bake at 275°F until cake tester inserted in the center comes out clean. Cool the cones and guide the preschoolers to ice them. Candy sprinkles may be added.

—Submitted by Jullia Stiltner
Grundy, Virginia

Applesauce

Materials: 6-8 cooking apples, ¼ cup water, ½ cup sugar, ¼ teaspoon cinnamon, boiler and hot plate or electric skillet, water, plastic knives, and spoon

Guide the preschoolers to wash, peel, core, and cut up the apples. Place in the boiler or skillet. Help the preschoolers add the sugar, water, and cinnamon. Stir until the ingredients are mixed. Guide the preschoolers to watch the apples to be sure there is enough water. The adult will stir occasionally.

Cook until soft, about 20-30 minutes. Let preschoolers put the applesauce in dishes to taste or serve on graham crackers.

—Submitted by Carolyn Hatcher
Dunwoody, Georgia

Banana Smoothie

Materials: 4 tablespoons honey, 2 mashed bananas, 1 cup plain yogurt, 1 cup orange juice, several ice cubes, blender, and small cups

Guide the boys and girls to measure the above ingredients and place them in a blender. Mix for 15-20 seconds. Pour mixture into cups and serve.

Bananas and Granola

Materials: ½ banana per preschooler; 1 box granola; craft sticks; and shallow, disposable pans

Cut the peeled bananas in half. Guide each preschooler to insert a stick into half a banana. Place the granola in shallow pans. Lead the preschoolers to take turns rolling their bananas in the granola. They will enjoy this treat.

—Submitted by Cindy Kemp
Rockville, Maryland

Homemade Snowcone

Materials: ice crusher, blender, or food processor; 3-ounce paper cups; any flavor fruit juice; ice cubes; and plastic spoons

Guide the preschoolers to take turns putting ice in the blender to be crushed. Give each child a paper cup. Spoon crushed ice into the cups and pour juice over the ice. Suggest that preshoolers eat the snowcones with a spoon.

—Submitted by Robin Pennington
Tucson, Arizona

Easy Chocolate Ice Cream

Materials: 2 quarts chocolate milk; 1 9-ounce container whipped topping, thawed; 1 can sweetened condensed milk; ice cream freezer; ice; and ice cream salt

Lead the preschoolers to mix all ingredients except ice and salt. Freeze in ice cream freezer with ice and salt.

—Submitted by Christine McCauley
Tallahassee, Florida

No-Bake Oatmeal Cookies

Materials: ¾ cup sugar; 2 cups uncooked, quick oatmeal; ⅔ cup margarine; ½ teaspoon vanilla; 2 tablespoons cocoa; 1 tablespoon milk; confectioners sugar; red granulated sugar or chocolate shavings (optional); bowls; waxed paper; and spoon

Lead the preschoolers to take turns creaming the margarine. They may mix the sugar and cocoa and add to the margarine. Add vanilla, milk, and oatmeal. Let them shape the mixture into balls with clean hands. Roll the balls in confectioners sugar, red granulated sugar, or chocolate shavings.

—Submitted by Mrs. R. L. Blaine
Bowling Green, Kentucky

Hot Chocolate Mix Gift Jars

Materials: ½-pint canning jars and lids; ¼ yard of calico; ribbon; 2-pound can instant chocolate drink powder; 8-quart box powdered milk; 1-pound box confectioners sugar; 11-ounce jar coffee creamer; large mixing bowl; mixing spoon; and instruction cards

Before the session, cut the calico into 6-inch circles. Measure and cut the ribbon to fit around the jar lid rings, leaving enough for a bow.
    Let the preschoolers pour the ingredients into a large bowl and mix. They may take turns stirring the mixture. Help the preschoolers fill the jars. Show them how to fit the calico circles over the lids and screw on the rings. Help them tie the ribbon around each ring. Attach a card which reads:
    ⅓ cup mix + 1 cup hot water = a warm treat for you.
    This may be used as a gift. Provide self-sealing bags for preschoolers to take home a sample of the mix.

—Submitted by Sue M. Perry
Gulfport, Mississippi

Orange Juice Drink

Materials: 1 6-ounce can frozen orange juice, 1 cup milk, 1 teaspoon vanilla, ½ cup sugar, blender, and paper cups

Allow the preschoolers to add ingredients to the blender. Blend together about 30 seconds. This is very rich. The amount of sugar may be decreased and a little water added, if desired.

—Submitted by Lynda B. Mills
Pasadena, Texas

Kenyan Corn Cakes

Materials: electric skillet; corn muffin mix, plus ingredients listed on box; bowl; spoon; spatula; measuring cup; margarine; tablespoon; and napkins

Lead preschoolers to place the mix and other ingredients in the bowl and stir. Heat the margarine in the skillet. Use one or two tablespoons of batter for each small cake. The teacher cooks the mix as pancakes, turning once when top is dry and edges are bubbly.

Tell preschoolers that corn is also eaten in other ways in Kenya, roasted, as mush, and mixed with beans. It is one of the main foods eaten in Kenya.

Graham-Cracker Balls

Materials: 1 cup confectioners sugar, 3-ounce package cream cheese, 2 tablespoons cocoa, 2½ cups crushed graham crackers, 1 tablespoon grated orange rind, 2 tablespoons light corn syrup, ¼ cup orange juice, plastic mixing bowl, wooden spoon, and waxed paper

Start with a warm bowl and have the cream cheese at room temperature. Lead the preschoolers to measure and add the other ingredients. Let them mix the sugar and cocoa and combine with the cracker crumbs. Add the orange rind and remind them to stir well to blend ingredients. Add the corn syrup and juice, mixing thoroughly. Preschoolers may use clean hands to roll the mixture into small balls. Place balls on waxed paper.

—Submitted by Cris Williamson
Macon, Georgia

Enrichment Ideas

"Will it be fun?"

Book for Infants and Creepers

Materials: cardboard, notebook rings, colorful pictures, clear self-adhesive plastic, glue, and hole punch

Cut the cardboard into the desired size for pages. Paste pictures on the cardboad pieces. Cover the pages with clear self-adhesive plastic. Punch holes. Place rings through the holes to make a book.

—*Submitted by Jeroline Baker*
Fort Worth, Texas

Enrichment Ideas

Fishing

Materials: a large refrigerator box; old fishing pole or dowel; string; paper fish; a magnet; utility knife; and paper clips

Ahead of time, cut two canoe shapes from the large box. Place a child-size chair at each end in between the two cardboard canoes.

To make a fishing pole, use an old one, without the hook. Or, use dowel stick with a string attached. Put a magnet on the end of the string. Cut out paper fish and put a paper clip where the mouth is. The magnet on the fishing pole will pick up the paper clip on the fish.

This fishing activity will enhance dramatic play when placed with blocks.

—Submitted by Linda Graham
Raytown, Missouri

Cut a canoe from each side of box

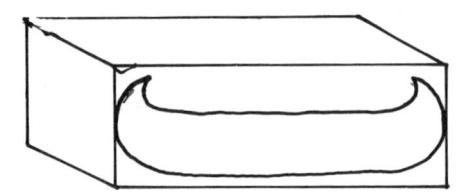

Changeable Mobile

Materials: plastic margarine container lids; black felt-tip markers; and string

On three plastic lids, draw a simple human face using the black felt-tip markers. Suspend the lids, mobile fashion, face-down so the infant can watch each face as it moves when bumped. Stark black and white colors are best for the youngest infants. Progress to pictures cut from magazines as the child gets older. Change the pictures often.

—Submitted by Anne H. Smith
Louisville, Kentucky

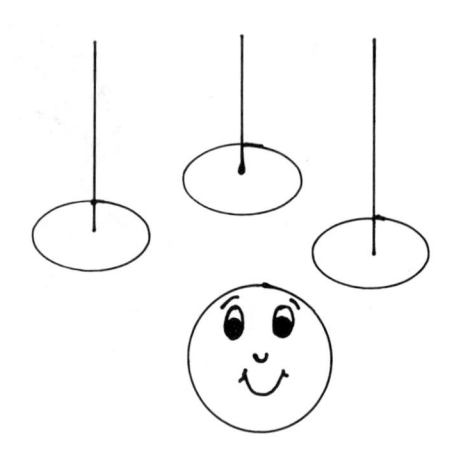

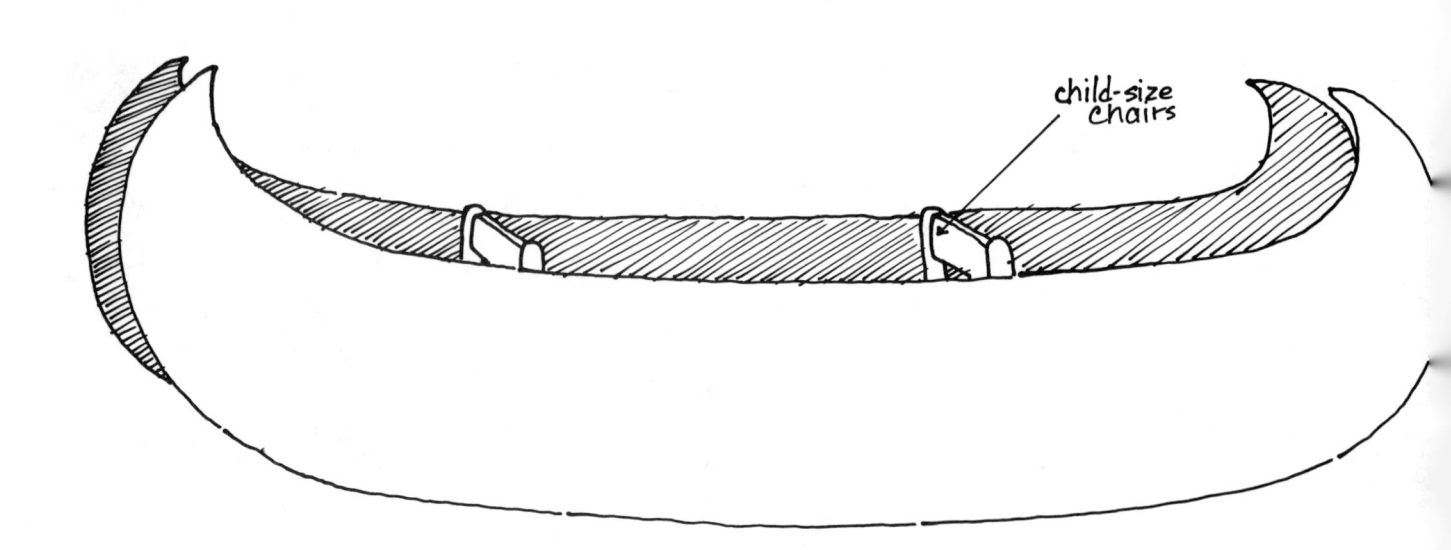

child-size chairs

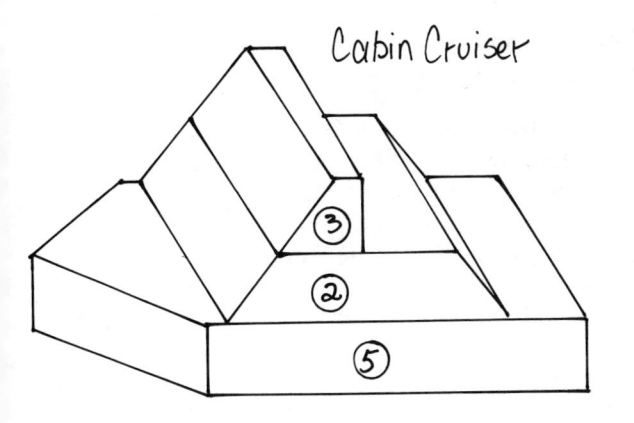

Wooden Tugboat, Cabin Cruiser, and Van

Materials: white pine board, three-quarter-inch thick; three-quarter-inch dowels; three-quarter-inch roofing nails or tacks; number four nails, one-and-one-half-inches long; white glue; saw; and hammer

See illustrations for pieces to cut from the board for each item. Assemble with white glue, except for the wheels, which are attached with nails.

—*Submitted by Roy Dawson*
Albuquerque, New Mexico

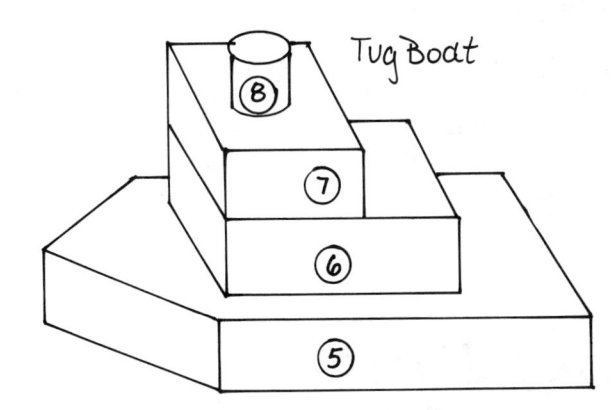

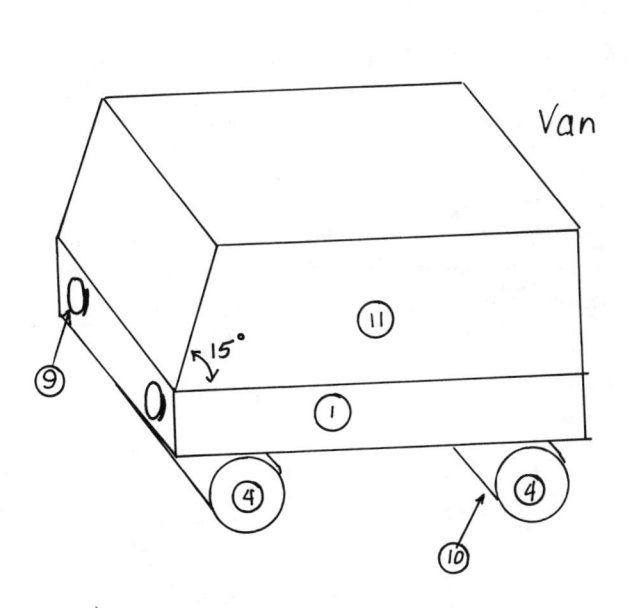

Enrichment Ideas

Cabin Cruiser

Tug Boat

Van

1 inch pine (¾ inch thick)

① 2" x 4½"
② 2" x 3"
③ 2" x 1½"
⑤ 2" x 5½"
⑥ 1½" x 2¾"
⑦ 1½" x 1½"
⑪ 1½" x 2" x 4½"

¾ inch dowel

④ 2" long (pre-drilled for nails)
⑧ ¾" long

Nails

⑨ ¾" long roofing nail (or tacks)
⑩ #4 nail, 1½" long

Enrichment Ideas

City Scene

Materials: twin-size flat white sheet; tube paint; assorted boxes, covered with newsprint; and small toy vehicles to roll on the scene

Before a session, draw roads, a park, a river, an airport, and city blocks onto the sheet. Then paint with washable tube paints. Leave the city blocks plain so that preschoolers can add box buildings. Make the roads the size of the small three- to four-inch long cars and trucks.

At the session, spread the sheet on the floor and pretend it is any city that you are studying. If the floor is carpeted, Velcro attached to the back of the sheet will help it lay flat.

The preschoolers may help cover the boxes with newsprint or construction paper and draw building features on them. These may be placed as the preschoolers wish on the city scene.

—Submitted by Linda Graham
Raytown, Missouri

Fence

Materials: plastic fruit or vegetable baskets, twist ties, and scissors

The teacher cuts the sides from the plastic baskets. Show the preschoolers how to use twist ties to connect the basket-sides together to make a fence or a corral for animals.

—Submitted by Johanna Dawson
Albuquerque, New Mexico

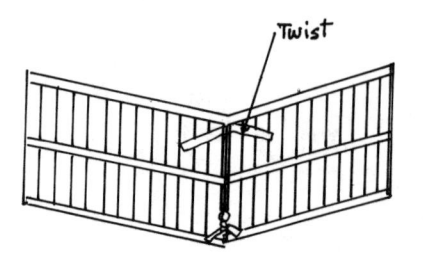

Writing a Story

Materials: large sheets of newsprint or lined flip chart and felt-tip marker

Initiate conversation about an experience the preschoolers have had. Say: Let's write a story.
  Explain the parts of the story: beginning, what happened next, the end. As each child gives a sentence, record it on the newsprint. When the story is finished, read it to the class. Then tape it to the wall so the preschoolers can "read" their story.

—Submitted by Peggy Jones
Baltimore, Maryland

Design Board

Materials: five-by-five-inch square of wood, 25 nails, and rubber bands

Hammer nails in five evenly-spaced rows of five nails each. Nails should be the same height. The child stretches rubber bands around the nails to make patterns, shapes, and designs.

—Submitted by Sharon B. Garnett
Chesapeake, Virginia

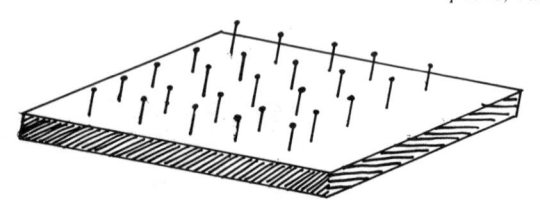

Quiet Book

Materials: quilted fabric, unbleached muslin, felt, liquid embroidery, snaps, zipper, thread, Velcro, buttons, and various sewing notions as desired

Make the cover from quilted fabric, lined with muslin. Cut the pages from muslin. Cut out designs from the felt to make a picture book which has zippers, snaps, buttons, etc. to help a preschooler develop skills in handling these items.

Changeable Book for Younger Preschoolers

Materials: large self-sealing bags; hole punch; 42-44-inch shoestring (one per book); and pictures mounted on poster board, cardboard, or construction paper

Put together five or six self-sealing bags with the zippers at the top. Punch two rows of holes on the left side of the bags and lace the shoestring through the holes. Place the pictures in the bags and seal the zippers.

This type of homemade book allows babies, creepers, and toddlers to use books and then for teachers to sterilize them. Also, with the zippers at the top, the pictures may be changed to make new books.

—Submitted by Kathy Sapp
Pineville, Louisiana

Double each piece of fabric, forming one double page. Sew on all designs before assembling the book. Examples of pages are: pants to zip; girl with jumper or blouse to button; shoe or skate to lace and tie; shapes and colors to match using Velcro; a purse to snap and unsnap.

—Submitted by Lucy Stewart
Louisville, Kentucky

Plastic Book for Younger Preschoolers

Materials: four or five plastic lids; pictures of families, animals, etc.; clear self-adhesive plastic; one large notebook ring; and hole punch

Use four or five plastic lids for book covers and pages. Glue pictures to the lids. Cover each picture with clear self-adhesive plastic so pictures can be kept clean. Punch a hole in each lid and fasten them together with the notebook ring. This book may be used with younger preschoolers since it can be cleaned and kept sanitary, plus the pages will not tear.

—Submitted by Dorothy Thayer Jones
Midwest City, Oklahoma

Photograph-Album Book for Young Ones

Materials: photograph album with magnetic pages and pictures of nature, family, community helpers, etc.

Cut out the colorful pictures. Place one picture under the plastic of each page of the photo album. A separate book may be made for each subject. Place the title or subject on the outside spine of the book. These can be stored flat with the spines facing out.

—Submitted by Jeroline Baker
Fort Worth, Texas

Helpers-at-Church Book

Materials: church directory, cardboard, plastic notebook rings, glue, scissors, hole punch, and clear self-adhesive plastic

Cut out the pictures of the church staff from the church directory. Glue the pictures on cardboard. Cover with clear, self-adhesive plastic. Punch holes on the left edge, and secure with plastic rings.

—Submitted by Anne H. Smith
Louisville, Kentucky

Push and Crawl Toy: Roly-Poly

Materials: a plastic soft-drink bottle; sharp knife; glue; waterproof mailing tape; and rocks, shells, bells, or colored balls

Use the knife to cut off the top one-fourth of the bottle. Separate the remaining clear plastic bottle from the black plastic bottom. Put the shells, bells, rocks, or balls inside the clear end. Apply glue to the cut edge. Place the open end inside the black bottom piece. Seal with tape. Push the toy to entice a creeper to crawl after it.

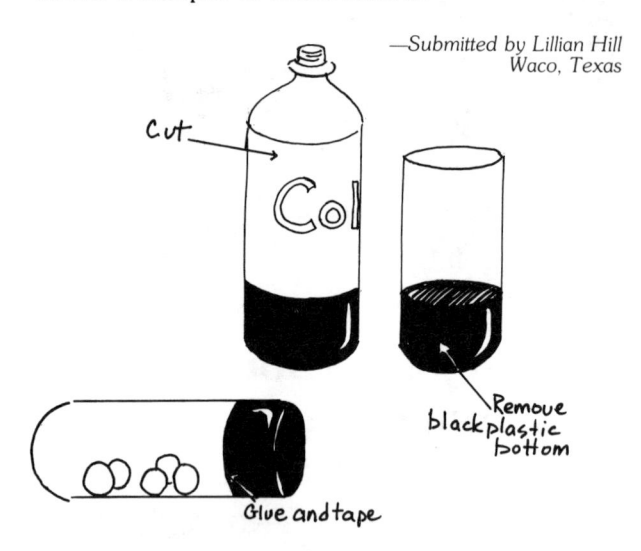

—Submitted by Lillian Hill
Waco, Texas

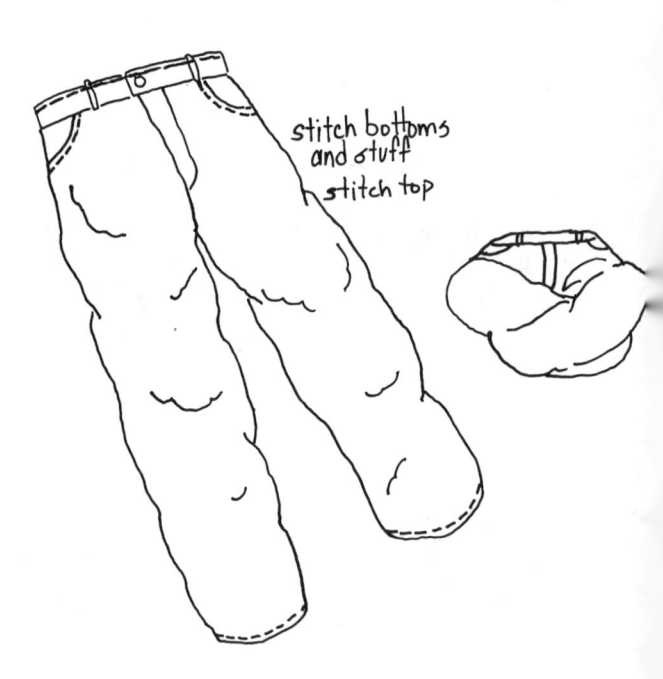

Christmas Water Toy

Materials: clear plastic detergent bottle, green food coloring, gold or silver sequins, and gold or silver bells

Rinse the bottle and fill it with water. Add green food coloring to the water. Put the gold and silver sequins and the bells in the water. Glue the top on and tape it. This is a toy babies, creepers, and toddlers enjoy.

—Submitted by Brenda Dedmon
Snellville, Georgia

Jeans Chair

Materials: old pair of jeans, Styrofoam packing materials, sewing maching, and thread

Stitch the legs of the jeans closed at the bottom. Loosely stuff the jeans with the packing material. Stitch the top of the jeans closed. Use as a sit-upon.

—Submitted by Linda Wayne
Ozark, Alabama

Beginning Sounds

Materials: newsprint, construction paper, magazines, catalogs, scissors, glue, and felt-tip marker

Write a letter of the alphabet in the center of a piece of newsprint. Instruct the preschoolers to look for pictures of things that begin with the sound of that letter and to cut out the pictures. Then they can paste the pictures on the newsprint around the letter.

As an alternate activity, talk about an activity area in the room, and let the prescoolers cut out pictures of items used in that area. For example, homeliving would have kitchen items, table, chairs, food, play dough, etc., included in it.

—Submitted by Elsie M. McCall
Mill Valley, California

Match Shape Silhouettes

Materials: a small, square box; a rectangular shoe box; a round oatmeal box; construction-paper shapes cut the same size as the box bottoms; and masking tape

Tape the paper silhouettes of the box shapes to the floor in the block area. Place the matching boxes on the floor near the shapes. Show preschoolers how to match the box to the shape. Allow creative play, if preschoolers prefer to use the boxes for stacking or building.

—Submitted by Lillian Hill
Waco, Texas

Homemade Bubbles

Materials: four tablespoons liquid soap, four tablespoons water, two tablespoons liquid starch, and bowl or jar

Mix the ingredients, and shake well. The preschoolers use straws, plastic wands, or spools to blow bubbles.

—Submitted by Selma Johnson
Shreveport, Lousiana

Paint Smock

Materials: plastic trash-can liner, scissors, and spring-type clothespin

To make an inexpensive, practical smock to use for art activities, use a plastic bag. Cut the neck from the bottom of the bag. Open one side of the bag by cutting from the opening to the neck portion. Cut two holes for the arms to go through. Fasten the smock in the back with masking tape or a clothespin.

Racquet and Ball

Materials: metal coat hanger, panty hose, yarn, cardboard (small square piece), and scissors

Racquet: Bend the hanger into a diamond shape, rounded at the top. Stretch the hose over the hanger and wrap the extra around the bottom to cushion the hook. Wrap with yarn to secure the hose.
Ball: Wrap yarn loosely around the cardboard. Wrap enough times to give the ball some bulk. Take out the cardboard, tie a piece of yarn around the center, and clip the ends.
  These may be used by one child to bounce the ball on the racquet. Two preschoolers may bat the ball back and forth to one another.

—Submitted by Gail Skipper Guyton
New Orleans, Lousiana

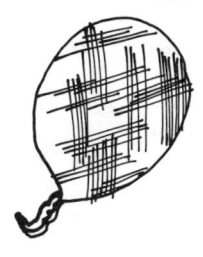

Peekaboo Board

Materials: 12-by-12-inch cardboard, scissors, and colorful self-adhesive plastic

Cover the cardboard with the self-adhesive plastic. Cut a square, circle, and triangle shape, leaving a hinge to attach each to the board. As a baby lays on his stomach, place the board between you. Surprise the baby by opening one shape to let him see your face. Peekaboo is always enjoyable for an infant.

—Submitted by Anne H. Smith
Louisville, Kentucky

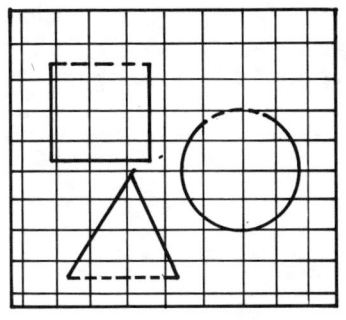

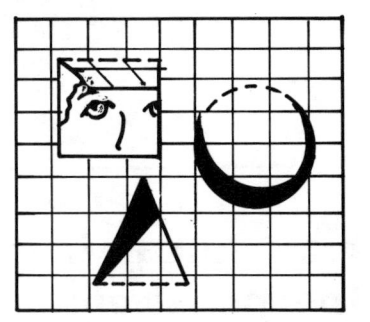

Mobile for Creepers and Toddlers

Materials: beach ball, ten feet of yarn or string, and tack or eye-screw

Inflate the beach ball. Tie the string around the valve. Hang the ball from the ceiling with the tack or eye-screw so that it hangs about six inches from the floor.
  Creepers will enjoy crawling toward and touching the ball. Toddlers will enjoy hitting at the ball to make it swing back and forth. The ball is so light that creepers and toddlers do not get hurt even if it swings into them. This mobile is *not* suitable for twos and older.

Enrichment Ideas

69

Enrichment Ideas

Easel (for limited budget and space)

Materials: scrap of wood 40-by-15 inches, roll of narrow newsprint, old towel or plastic tablecloth, cans of assorted sizes, yarn, blunt scissors, felt-tip marker, paint, brushes, and child's chair

Spread towel on floor. Place newsprint on floor by wall. Lean wood against the wall over the newsprint. Pull newsprint up and over the board so that it flops over the front. Place chair in front of board. Set large can on chair with smaller can of paint and a brush inside. Attach yarn pieces to scissors and marker. Hang scissors on right for cut-off. Hang marker on left to write name.

—Submitted by Connie Markham
Montpelier, Vermont

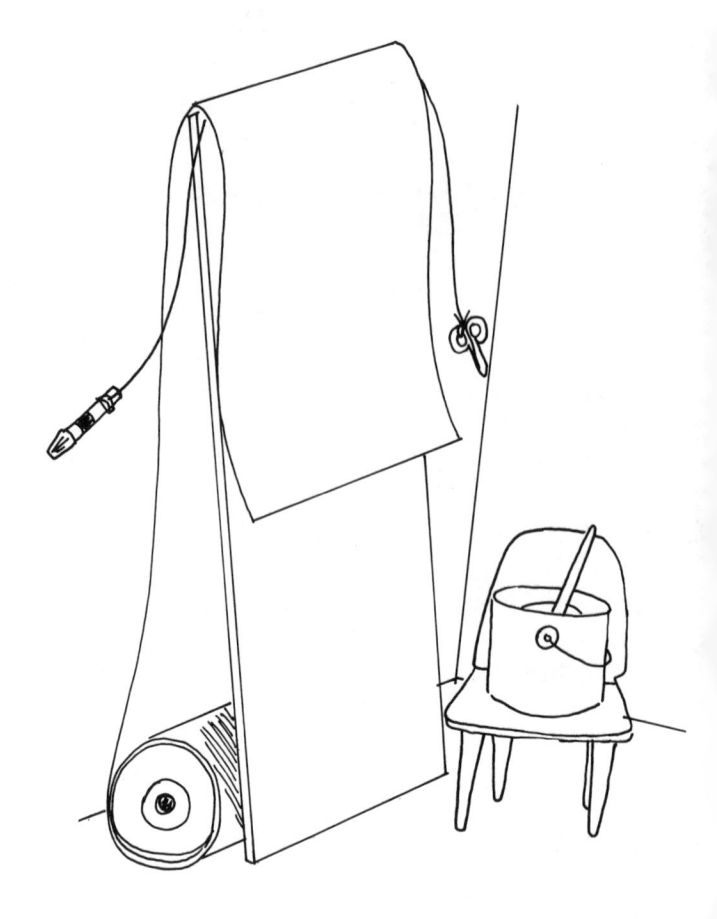

How to Laminate Inexpensively

Materials: laminating film (from school supply stores); iron; scissors, protected surface on which to iron; and materials to be laminated

Preserving games and visuals with laminating film can be easier and less expensive than using clear, self-adhesive plastic.

Cut a piece of laminating film a little larger than the paper to be covered. Place the film on the paper, shiny side up. Part of the film will hang over the edge, so place a cloth or laminated poster board underneath the work.

Use a dry iron, set low in the permanent-press range. Press the film to the paper, beginning in the center and pressing toward the edge. Trim off the excess film. Use the iron to touch up any loose spots around the edges.

—Submitted by Nell Branum
Mount Olive, Alabama

Handy Picture File

Materials: manila folders, file box, and pictures

Clip pictures from magazines, quarterlies, and other sources. File by subjects, such as people, preschoolers, community helpers, families, church, etc.

—Submitted by Lucy Stewart
Louisville, Kentucky

Workbench Substitute

Materials: a short, wide piece of tree trunk, large nails with heads, and a hammer

Place the stump on the floor in an out-of-the-way spot. Provide hammer and nails. This is an amazingly quiet activity considering the energy level involved.

—Submitted by Connie Markham
Montpelier, Vermont

The Street Where I Go to Church

Materials: old window shade and permanent felt-tip markers

Use the felt-tip markers to draw the streets in the area of your church on the shade. Place the shade on the floor in the block area. The preschoolers build the neighborhood with their blocks and drive through it with their cars. Shades can be rolled back up and stored for later use.

—Submitted by Brenda Dedmon
Snellville, Georgia

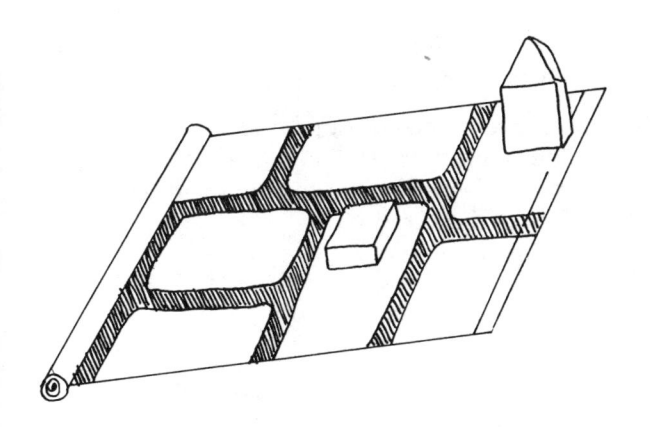

Listening Glasses

Materials: an old pair of glasses or sunglasses, felt fabric or self-adhesive plastic; scraps of braid and trim; scissors; and glue

Many listening games and activities require that participants close their eyes or be blindfolded. Some preschoolers are afraid of a blindfold and have trouble keeping their eyes closed. The teacher may make a pair of "Listening Glasses" to use for games.
  Glue felt (or use self-adhesive plastic) over the lenses of the glasses. Glue on braid, trim, small pompoms, etc., to decorate the glasses.

—Submitted by Nell Branum
Mount Olive, Alabama

Doll Cradle

Materials: oatmeal box, utility knife, scissors, tempera paint or colorful self-adhesive plastic, glue

Cut the oatmeal box in half from the bottom to three-fourths of the way up. Glue on the lid. The preschooler may paint the outside of the cradle or cover it with a colorful self-adhesive plastic.

—Submitted by Anne H. Smith
Louisville, Kentucky

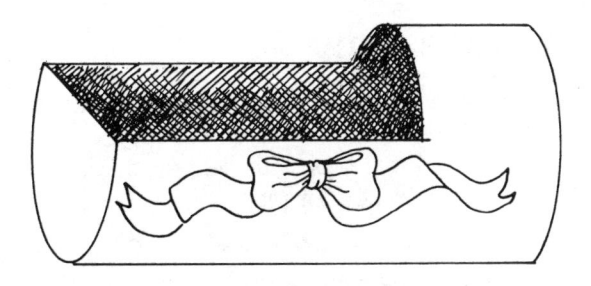

Matching Block Patterns

Materials: index cards and colored one-inch cube blocks

Draw block designs on index cards. Let the preschoolers enjoy making arrangements with their blocks to match the patterns on the cards.

—Submitted by Sharon B. Garnett
Chesapeake, Virginia

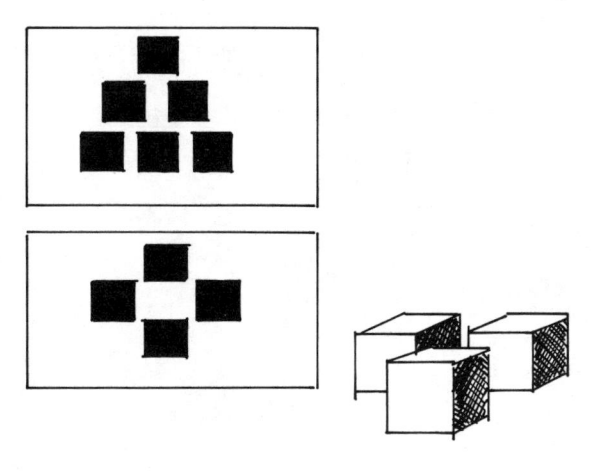

Enrichment Ideas

Toe Toucher

Materials: elastic cord, several large paper clips, and assorted objects of various textures

Stretch the cord across the baby's crib (about where the baby's feet would be) and tie to the rails on either side. From the clips hang items, such as a feather; small, stuffed furry toy; and a piece of foam. Place the barefoot baby in the crib so he can touch the objects with his toes as he kicks.

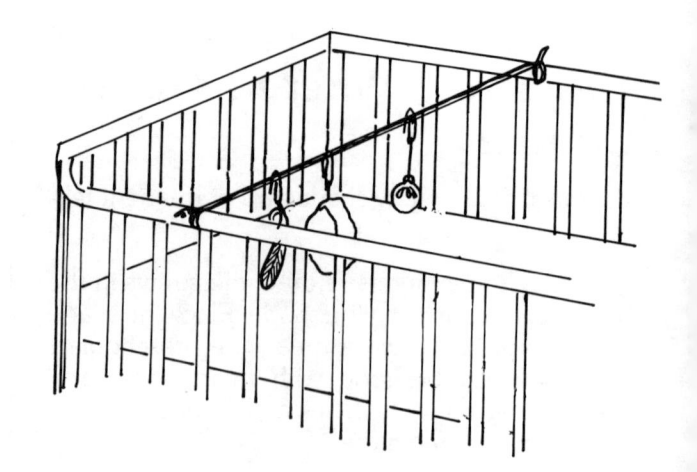

—Submitted by Anne H. Smith
Louisville, Kentucky

Treasure Box

Materials: construction paper of any color or colorful self-adhesive plastic; one empty, round, one-pound oatmeal box with lid per child; scissors; glue; and stickers or pictures

Measure the paper around the box. Cover the box and lid with the paper and glue. Put the child's name on the lid. Let each preschooler decorate his box with stickers or pictures. Each child now has a treasure box.

—Submitted by Jullia Stiltner
Grundy, Virginia

Storage Boxes

Materials: empty cereal boxes, any size; and colorful self-adhesive plastic

Cut the box diagonally from the top corner to approximately five inches from the bottom. Cover it with self-adhesive plastic. Label the box on the side. Excellent for storing recordings, magazines, pictures, etc.

—Submitted by Jane Taylor Howell
Owensboro, Kentucky

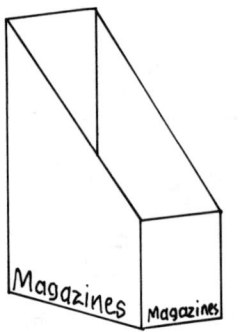

Let's Go Camping

Materials: large cardboard box, knife or scissors, and tape

Remove two opposite sides and the top of the box. The bottom will stay in place. Tape the two remaining sides to form a triangle. Cut windows in each side if desired.

—Submitted by Anne H. Smith
Louisville, Kentucky

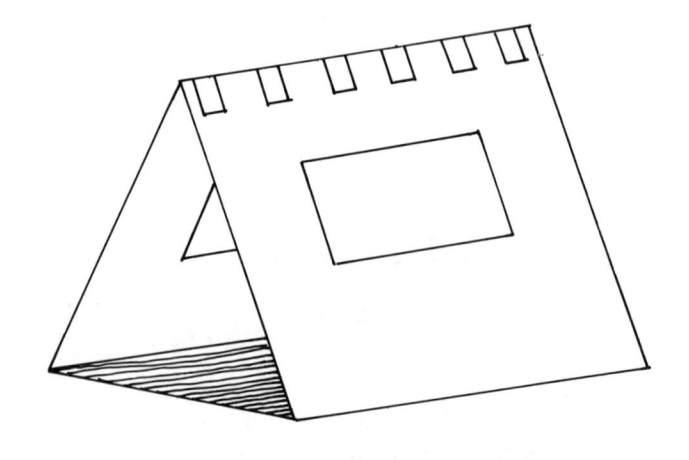